THE SECRET CAPTURE

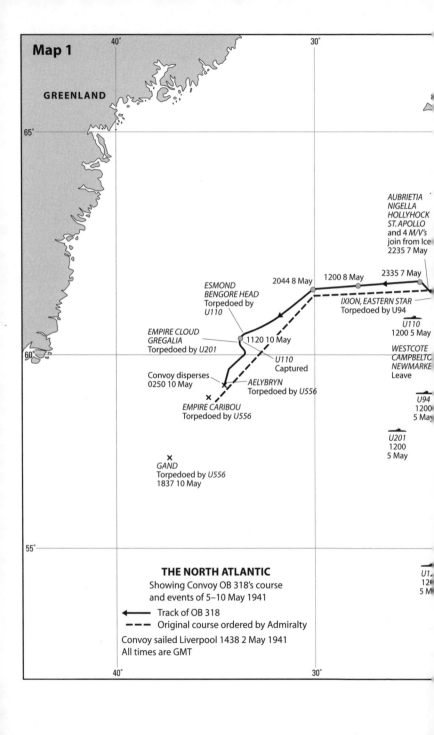

Map 1

GREENLAND

40°

30°

65°

60°

55°

AUBRIETIA
NIGELLA
HOLLYHOCK
ST. APOLLO
and 4 M/V's
join from Ice
2235 7 May

2044 8 May   1200 8 May   2335 7 May

ESMOND
BENGORE HEAD
Torpedoed by
U110

IXION, EASTERN STAR
Torpedoed by U94

U110
1200 5 May

EMPIRE CLOUD
GREGALIA
Torpedoed by U201   1120 10 May

WESTCOTE
CAMPBELTO
NEWMARKE
Leave

U110
Captured

Convoy disperses
0250 10 May

AELYBRYN
Torpedoed by U556

×
EMPIRE CARIBOU
Torpedoed by U556

U94
1200
5 May

U201
1200
5 May

×
GAND
Torpedoed by U556
1837 10 May

THE NORTH ATLANTIC
Showing Convoy OB 318's course
and events of 5–10 May 1941

U1
12
5 M

◄─── Track of OB 318
- - - Original course ordered by Admiralty

Convoy sailed Liverpool 1438 2 May 1941
All times are GMT

40°   30°

20°

10°

ICELAND

N

65°

Hvalfiord
Reykjavik

rd ESCORT
ROUP
ULLDOG
MAZON
ROADWAY
ANPURA
oin 1735

Faeröe
Islands

ESCORT
WESTCOTE
ROCHESTER
CAMPBELTOWN
NEWMARKET
MARIGOLD
PRIMROSE
NASTURTIUM
DIANTHUS
AURICULA
ANGLE

200
May

Iceland section of
convoy leaves

U96
1200 5 May

U556
1200 7 May

U143
1200
5 May

oat first
ating report

German aircraft reports
a convoy (SC 29) in this
area 0630 6 May

Bill Baileys
Bank

1200
6 May

1200
5 May

Hudson 0/269
× attacks U141

60°

U95
1200
5 May

U141
1200
5 May

Butt of
Lewis

Cape Wrath

Wick

Hebrides

Minches

· Rockall

1200
4 May

SCOTLAND

N O R T H

A T L A N T I C

55°

O C E A N

U75
1200
5 May

Irish
Sea

IRELAND

Liverpool

20°

10°

The
SECRET CAPTURE

CAPTAIN S W ROSKILL DSC RN

New Introduction by Professor Barry Gough

New Foreword by Charles Baker-Cresswell

Naval Institute Press
ANNAPOLIS, MARYLAND

This book is dedicated to
Captain Addison Joe Baker-Cresswell, DSO, RN,
and to the Officers and Men
of the 3rd Escort Group

This edition first published in Great Britain in 2011 by
Seaforth Publishing,
Pen & Sword Books Ltd,
47 Church Street,
Barnsley S70 2AS

Published and distributed in the
United States of America and Canada by the
Naval Institute Press,
291 Wood Road, Annapolis,
Maryland 21402-5034

www.nip.org

Library of Congress Control Number: 2010941901

ISBN 978 1 59114 810 4

This edition authorized for sale only in the United States of America,
its territories and possessions, and Canada

Printed and bound in Great Britain

CONTENTS

MAPS

DIAGRAMS

New Foreword

THE CENTRAL figure in this story, A J Baker-Cresswell (my father) was born in London in 1901. Queen Victoria was also in London then, but she was dead and would be buried at Windsor the following day.

My father grew up to become a good mathematician and chose the Royal Navy for his career. He specialised as a navigator. In the late 1920s the Navy kept two sloops based at Auckland, New Zealand. Their purpose was to suppress cannibalism in the Pacific Islands. He was posted to one of these sloops. It was in Auckland that he found his bride – he married her there when she was nineteen. On their return to England, they set up their home in the Meon Valley in Hampshire. By the time I was born – the youngest of their three children – he was navigating officer of HMS *Rodney*, and it was on board her that I was christened.

When World War II broke out, he was entirely ready for it. He was Staff College trained and had plenty of sea-going experience. He was the complete professional – one of a breed that the Navy had produced in enviable numbers.

During the war my mother and my two elder sisters saw him hardly at all. We watched the dogfights in the skies above the Hampshire Downs and came to recognise the peculiar undulating engine noise of German bombers at night. My mother had a touching faith in the ability of the dining-room table to shelter us from the bombs when the raids got too close, but she had bought a .22 with which to shoot German paratroopers. So we knew there was plenty of danger about and we heard of battles far away.

We also knew that my father was in the thick of it, and we knew *when* my father was awarded the DSO – but had no idea *why* until years later.

My mother once described to me how she had received a garbled message that HMS *Bulldog*, his ship, would be docking at Liverpool for repairs. Through the blackout and the irregularity of wartime trains she arrived there during an air raid and booked in at the Adelphi Hotel. She described walking to the docks with fires still blazing and stepping over criss-crossed fire hoses which jetted water from their punctures. She never found *Bulldog*, nor her husband, so simply made her difficult way back to Hampshire.

Sixty years later I found his little leather bound Letts diary, only three inches by two-and-a-half and still with its blunt pencil pushed down the spine. It is for the year 1941. This was his year of commanding 3rd Escort Group from HMS *Bulldog*. On 9 January he notes 'Assume command'. It gives details in the briefest form of all his convoys that he escorted. Most of the entries involve Greenock, Loch Ewe, Hvalfiord and Reykjavik.

A typical entry would be:

3 April	0800	Leave OB303
	1400	Arrive Hvalfiord
	1900	Arrive Reykjavik
	2230	Sail with 'Richmond Hill'
4 April	1400	Join HX116 (29 ships)

OB convoys were OUTWARD BOUND: HX meant they assembled off Halifax, Nova Scotia. Occasionally there were lists of his escorts.

12 July	0600	Sail
	1000	Off Campbeltown
	1530	Met OB 345
		'Nigella' 'Aubrietia' 'St Apollo' 'Notts County' 'King Sol' 'Daneman' 'Amazon' 'Georgetown'

Several of these were armed trawlers – the bravest of the brave. Think of them in this entry – one of several like it:

'1 February. N gale. Hove to for fourteen hours. Lost convoy.'
'4 February. S gale. Hove to twenty hours.'

Bad enough in a destroyer or a corvette with an open bridge but what about the trawlers?

I counted 28 convoys from January to October: 159 days at sea in that time, and no leave. Think of those days for all the men – both escorts and escorted. Days and long nights of constant danger, cold, tiredness, responsibility, discomfort, loneliness – and fear.

He reported the central action of this book in this way:

7 May 1941	0200	Sail
	1800	Join OB 318
		U-Boat attack
8 May		Re-join convoy
9 May	1200	Attack on convoy
	1245	Captured U-110
10 May	1100	U-110 sank
11 May	0100	Arrive Hvalfiord

A few days later:

15 May	1330	Arrive Hvalfiord
16 May		Fish with Aitken
		3lb sea trout
17 May		Fish with Roper
		3 trout, one char

He never wasted words.

David Balme was the gallant young officer who led the armed boat's crew on its perilous mission from *Bulldog*. My father kept his friendship with him to the end. I noticed that even when David was staying with him and was over sixty years old my father tended still to treat him as if he was a rash young Sub-Lieutenant of twenty.

'When you take him to Berwick Station,' he would say, 'make sure he gets onto the right platform.' 'But Father, there are only two platforms, and he knows where South is.' 'Never mind, make sure.'

The North Atlantic was by no means his only battlefield. He fought all the King's enemies: Vichy French, Italian, German and Japanese. I have in front of me his medals: DSO, Atlantic Star, Africa Star, Burma Star. He disapproved of sloppy dress. He described to me how he took a ship from Alexandria to Malta. During the day he fought the bombers of the Italian Air Force. Then he would go below for his supper, change into 'Mess Undress' and return to the bridge with a cigar, to fight the night battle against the Italian torpedo boats.

He died in 1997, aged 96. His New Zealand wife of seventy years died two weeks later. They are buried together in Bamburgh churchyard in his beloved Northumberland 100 yards from where I write.

CHARLES BAKER-CRESSWELL

November 2010

New Introduction

WITH HIS *The War at Sea* nearing completion (three volumes in four, 1954-1961) – undertaken while in the employ of the Cabinet Office under the direction of Professor Sir James Butler in the Military History Series – Captain Stephen Roskill, DSC, RN (Retd.) accepted an invitation from the publishers Collins to write a number of works in naval history and maritime affairs.[1] The book reprinted here for the first time in this welcome edition was one of these works. It first appeared in March 1959; there was a second impression a month later, and a German translation appeared in 1960. Its success was further proof of the author's outstanding capabilities as an historian and, equally important, his undeniable popularity with the reading public.

For his *War at Sea*, Roskill had consulted Commander Michael G Saunders in the Translation Division of the Admiralty Historical Section concerning German naval strategy and operations, and he was drawn to passages in Dönitz's 1939 book *Die U-Bootswaffe*. The German U-boat chief held that the destruction of the enemy's trade and the attack on his sea communications to be the true objectives of naval warfare. The First World War, the German admiral believed, demonstrated the effectiveness of the U-boats in trade warfare. Saunders thought Dönitz too reductionist but he had no doubt about the main theme, adding 'it is a sad thought that the British Naval Staff appeared in the interwar years largely to ignore these fundamental truths.'[2] For his description of German naval strategy Roskill had a useful summary (JIC 46 (33)) at his disposal and *Fuehrer Conferences on Naval Affairs 1939–1945.* All of these provided the background understanding for 'the secret capture'. He did not interview German survivors of the episode but he did have correspondence with various persons in the Royal Navy who knew of the event or were otherwise involved in it. Roskill wished to keep the story a British one, and as will now be explained sought to make clear to the widening English-speaking world reading the naval history of the Second World War that the Royal Navy had made a significant contribution to the winning of the war by 'the secret capture'.

Two years earlier, in 1957, the British publishers Sidgwick and Jackson published a book by Rear-Admiral Daniel V Gallery, USN, entitled *We Captured a U-Boat.* The work was a publishing success. When in command of USS *Pillsbury* in June 1944, a destroyer escort, Gallery had sent a boarding party to the foundering *U-505*. The submarine was saved from sinking and the party retrieved an Enigma coding machine and current code books. *U-505* was towed triumphantly into Bermuda. Gallery claimed that his was the only U-boat capture on the high seas. But in fact this was not the case. *U-570* surrendered to a Sunderland flying boat in 1941. Other attempts came close, including the Royal Canadian Navy's of 10 September 1941. In this event, HMCS *Chambly* and HMCS *Moose Jaw* forced *U-501* to the surface, but she sank. On 30 October 1942 HMS *Petard* seized German coding material from a sinking *U-558* in the eastern Mediterranean. But Gallery had made a good literary job of it. Thus Roskill's goal was to disclose to the wider world that the Royal Navy had done its work 'more than three years before Gallery's men hoisted the Stars and Stripes above the Nazi's crooked cross on board *U-505*.' Roskill held that his relations with American naval officers were always excellent, which was true for the period after 1945 and notably when he was Deputy Director of Naval Intelligence. In short, Roskill did not seek to score points at Gallery's expense; he only wished to correct the record – and to tell what he could of a story hitherto largely unknown.

Roskill reconstituted the story of the capture and boarding of the *U-110* on 9 May 1941 on the basis of what he admitted was contained in 'one small file'. He was hamstrung by many limitations, not least the Official Secrets Act. From the current literature, based on research long after Roskill wrote his book, the story has been more fully told.[3] Remarkably, much has come to light, as is the case with HMS *Bulldog* and *U-110*. But before we recount that episode we need to be reminded of what Roskill said about the limitations he faced and which obliged him to admit that he had written a 'short account of perhaps the most important and far-reaching success achieved by our anti-submarine forces during the whole course of the last war....' But getting access to files kept under wraps was only one problem. It was linked to a second: the requirement and necessity of not exposing Ultra. 'Official historians, working on a brief drawn up soon after 1945, are mostly silent about Intelligence.' So wrote the historian and editor, Donald McLachlan, a retired naval officer, in his book *Room 39: Naval Intelligence in Action, 1939-45*.[4] 'In most volumes of the official history [in the Military Series] the word does not appear in the index. Only in the four volumes of *The War at Sea* can it be said that an effort is made to give credit and apportion blame to intelligence; perhaps because the author, Captain Stephen Roskill, had been a Deputy Director of Naval Intelligence and knew his way about an explosive field of activity.' McLachlan was favoured by the release of documents, and at the time he wrote his book the thirty-year rule about access to official files was about to be introduced. Roskill had no such advantage, and his book must be read with a full appreciation of the fact that he worked under many limitations.

The 'one small file' that Roskill used to reconstitute the story is now in The National Archives, Kew, Surrey, Adm 1/11133. Contained in it are: the report of proceedings of the commanding officer of HMS *Bulldog*, Captain Joe Baker-Cresswell, Senior Officer, 3rd Escort Group, and the report under the heading

'Boarding Primrose', being the account of twenty-year-old Sub-Lieutenant David E Balme, RN. The latter contains personal recollections of interest, for it was he who led the boarding party aboard *U-110*, codenamed Primrose by the British.

In the immediate months leading up to this episode U-boat command had lost a number of submarines and 'aces': Prien, Kretschmer and Schepke. The operational area of U-boats was therefore pressed farther west, near Iceland. At 1202 GMT on 9 May 1941 two ships of west-bound convoy OB 318 were torpedoed in position 60° 20' N 40° W. The British escorts, destroyers *Bulldog* (lead ship) and *Broadway* and the corvette *Aubrietia*, all made contact, and *Aubrietia*'s depth charge attack was a good one. At 1235 a conning tower was sighted, and fire was immediately opened by 4.7in, 3in, 2pdr pom-pom and stripped Lewis guns. One 3in shell struck the conning tower, and men were seen abandoning the submarine. The small arms fire continued. *Broadway* approached to ram but the submarine turned stern on to her. The British vessel dropped a depth charge close to the submarine's bow. Oil covered the water. As we now know, that submarine had come quickly to the surface, surprisingly so, in fact. Her depth meters were not functioning, her electric motors out of commission, and she was taking on water.

The U-boat commander, the noted 'ace' Kapitänleutnant Fritz-Julius Lemp, Knights Cross, was first to emerge from the conning tower, ordering his crew to evacuate as soon as possible. Between gun bursts from the British ships, the German officers and men made their way up and out and sought security in the cold Atlantic, hoping for rescue. Lemp was under the impression that the damage to his submarine was so extensive that it would sink, taking its secrets with it. He also had given orders to set scuttling charges; these had failed to detonate.[5]

From the bridge of the *Bulldog* no sign of a white flag could be seen. Baker-Cresswell ordered Balme and an armed whaler's crew (six seamen, one telegraphist and one stoker) bearing small arms as a boarding party. By the time the whaler was alongside the submarine the whole crew appeared to have jumped into the water. Balme, under orders to seize all books and anything that looked important, opened the conning tower hatch. He went down the ladder to the lower conning tower, made a further entrance and found himself unopposed in the U-boat. He and others of the boarding party faced unimaginable circumstances aboard the wallowing U-boat: an eerie silence, the ominous hissing of air, a motor that they could not control, the fear of the enemy possibly lurking behind a bulkhead, the worry that the scuttling-charges would go off, and much else. Throughout these desperate hours the British escorts were attacking U-boats with depth charges, and Balme's fear was that their explosions, which felt very close, would set off the detonating charges. The various rooms and compartments were searched, and chief among the prizes was an Enigma machine, which looked somewhat like a typewriter but one in which keystrokes lit up different letters which without a code book were incomprehensible to the British telegraphist who had gone on board the U-boat. Various code books and other materials were gathered up from the immense clutter of paper and debris. These items were all passed up and out of the submarine by human chain, and meanwhile the clock steadily advanced.

The material was safely passed to the *Bulldog* then taken to Scapa Flow and thence to Bletchley Park, where before long it was added to other sources employed by the Operations Intelligence Centre at the Admiralty for deploying naval assets. By this time the British had already broken the main German naval codes. On 4 March, in the Lofoten Islands raid, Enigma material was captured from the armed trawler *Krebs*. This helped Bletchley Park to break the whole of the traffic of April 1941 down to 10 May. On 7 May the weather ship *München* was captured. From these 'pinches' vital information was gleaned. Indeed, signals from *U-110* were able to be read before it was captured.

The treasures from *U-110* added confirming, parallel or associate details. More specifically, the secret capture gave the British entry into the German 'officer-only' signals and the *Kurzsignale* (the shortened code) both of which were of extreme importance.[6]

A word might be said here about the use of this 'special intelligence'.[7] The Admiralty's Operational Intelligence Centre was able to re-route convoys past U-boats and ship losses were dramatically reduced. Dönitz was baffled by this, and there were only two possible explanations, he said: either treachery or enemy knowledge, which he thought unlikely. Tankers, weather ships and supply ships were destroyed, and this reduced the capabilities of German surface raiders. It had, too, an effect on dealing with the great German surface ships, another story.[8] In larger measure, signals intelligence, and the breaking of the naval Enigma, was the most important single factor in the defeat of the U-boats in 1943. This 'first charge on the resources of the United Nations', as Churchill put it, was the 'prelude to all effective aggressive operations', notably the Allied invasion of Europe and after, and perhaps shortened the war from a probable 1947 to 1945.

The story of the secret capture is one of many episodes in the famed battle of the Atlantic. It will always be one of some mystery and even of literary romance, for the U-boat in question could not be saved. The thirty-two German submariners fortunate to have escaped an icy death never knew that their vessel had been captured and boarded; in consequence, they could not reveal any secrets that had been gathered from it.[9] The prisoners spent long years in captivity in Britain and in Canada. As for Lemp, he did not survive. He probably did not commit suicide, as has been imagined, though his first officer recounted that he did swim back towards his damaged but still-floating command, perhaps with a view to boarding and sinking; and he was not killed by gunfire. Most likely, he drowned in the rising sea, having been most successful in saving most of his ship's complement. His last words had been 'Leave everything. Leave everything. Get out, get out, get out!'[10] Against this is the record of Lemp; when in command of *U-30* on the first day of the war he sank the liner *Athenia*, an act of undoubted murder (there was a loss of 118) though one explained away by German high command. Lemp had thought the *Athenia* to be an armed merchant cruiser. In any event, he joined many another U-boat ace on the bottom of the ocean. Lemp had made ten patrols, a total of 235 days at sea. His successes were formidable: 19 ships sunk for a total of 96,314 GRT, 1 auxiliary warship sunk (325 GRT), 3 ships damaged (14,317 GRT) and 1 warship, the *Barham*, damaged (31,100 tons).

As for Baker-Cresswell, a modest fellow, he did not parade his successes. He was an excellent escort group leader. When his command was finished he sent this message to those under his immediate authority: 'good luck and good hunting.' Like Roskill he served as Deputy Director of Naval Intelligence. Then he became a justice of the peace, threw himself into good works, and enjoyed country sports, particularly fishing. But journalists and video producers kept calling at his door. He died in 1997, aged 96.

In 1988, at Christmas, in one of his last communications to David Balme, Baker-Cresswell made some lasting evaluations of significance of what had transpired on the ocean wastes in 1941:

> The whole beauty of our exploit was the providential timing of it. The situation was just about desperate at the time and if losses in the Atlantic had gone on increasingly at the same rate as in the beginning of 1941 we would probably have had to sue for peace.
>
> Churchill says it was the only thing he was really worried about and I remember thinking at the time that we could not go on. I think that my remark on the *Bulldog*'s bridge: By God! We'll do a *Magdeburg* [recovering a German code book as in 1914]! was as epoch-making as some of Churchill's sayings! Because, if we hadn't done a *Magdeburg*, our losses would have been insupportable.

Later it didn't matter so much because the Americans were in it and ships and aircraft were being turned out faster than they were being destroyed. Long after we are dead and gone, it will be written up again and the true lesson will be learnt. That breathing space we were given in 1941 when Rodger Winn in the Submarine Tracking Room was so clever with diverting convoys that we never got near a U-boat, was absolutely vital in the war. It is nice to think of the hundreds of ships and lives we saved, let alone the country.

On the sixtieth anniversary of Dönitz's capitulation as the second and last Führer, Balme donated Lemp's naval cap, salvaged when he took possession of Enigma. This relic of that remarkable undersea arm of the German Navy that terrorized the North Atlantic before it was swept from the seas is now an artifact in the Imperial War Museum, London. Lemp's Iron Cross, retrieved from *U-110*, Baker-Cresswell gave to Lemp's sister after the war.

Of 859 U-boats that conducted war patrols 648 were lost, and as Roskill put it unfailingly, the U-boat proved 'a source of anxiety to us right to the end'.[11] Though many have concluded that the battle of the Atlantic was won by the Allies by mid-1943, Roskill had a wiser appreciation: right to the dying days of the war, although dark clouds were gathering over the Third Reich and the U-boat arm, a stiff resistance was kept up until the last surrender was ordered from headquarters. In other words, the effectiveness and deployment of the Ultra secret was undoubtedly important in winning the battle at sea and perhaps shortened the war. But the resistance put up by a dogged and disadvantaged enemy was of remarkable strength. And the *U-110* episode was but one of countless battles that tested the equipment, resolve and capabilities of the sea fighters of the Second World War.

For assistance and materials used here I wish to thank Nicholas Roskill, Charles Baker-Cresswell, Margaret Griffiths of Bletchley

Park Trust, Ralph Erskine, Allen Packwood and the staff of the Churchill Archives Centre, and the Master and Fellows of Churchill College, Cambridge.

BARRY GOUGH
November 2010

Notes

1   For Roskill's engagement in this engaging and difficult enterprise and a bibliography of his works, see Barry Gough, *Historical Dreadnoughts: Arthur Marder, Stephen Roskill and Battles for Naval History* (Barnsley: Seaforth Publishing, 2010), 134-71, 341-2 respectively.

2   M.G. Saunders to Stephen Roskill, 18 September 1952, ROSK 4/47, Churchill Archives Centre.

3   Among many sources, see, in particular, Hugh Sebag-Montefiore, *Enigma: The Battle for the Code* (London: Weidenfeld & Nicolson, 2000), 131-45, David Kahn, *Seizing the Enigma: the Race to Break the German U-boat Codes, 1939-1943* (London: Arrow, 1996), 9-14, 161-68, and, more generally, Patrick Beesly, *Very Special Intelligence: The Story of the Admiralty's Operational Intelligence Centre, 1939-1945* (London: Hamish Hamilton, 1977) and F.H. Hinsley and Alan Stripp, eds., *Codebreakers: The Inside Story of Bletchely Park* (Oxford: Oxford University Press, 1993). On Anglo-American difficulties in sharing of intelligence secrets, see Dale Rielage, 'Indirectly in Operational Signals', *Naval History*, 16, 6 (December 2002): 31-35.

4   London: Weidenfeld & Nicolson, 1968. Quotations here are from pages xv and 99.

5   Obituary of Sir Barry Sheen, *The Sunday Times*, 27 October 2005. He was first lieutenant of *Aubrietia*, and was, while Balme was boarding the U-boat, interrogating German survivors. He later became a judge, and gave the verdict on the Zeebrugge ferry disaster, 1987, blaming the captain, first officer and owners of the *Herald of Free Enterprise*.

6   The official historian adds: 'but the Home Waters settings taken from her were those for April, of which most of the traffic had already been deciphered, and those for June, which duplicated the *München* material.' F.H. Hinsley *et al.*, *British Intelligence in the Second World War, 1* (*London*: HMSO, 1979), 337-38.

7   Of particular importance is Ralph Erskine, 'Naval Enigma: A Missing Link', *International Journal of Intelligence and Counterintelligence*, 3, 4 (1989): 493-508.

8   See Peter Jervis, *The German Battleships* (Bletchley, n.d.), 5-7.

9   Sixteen German sailors perished in this episode.

10 Many fresh details from the British and especially German side have been recounted in Andrew Williams, *The Battle of the Atlantic: Hitler's Gray Wolves of the Sea and the Allies' Desperate Struggle to Defeat them*. New York: Basic Books, 2003. This book accompanies the documentary series of the History Channel. There have been several video productions on the capture of *U-110*, British and American. Hollywood produced *U-505*, but that is a story for another day.

11 Roskill, *War at Sea*, 3, pt.2, 305. Roskill gives a figure of 785 U-boats lost in total; 126 of these were stated as lost by bombing or 'other causes'. Ibid., 472.

Foreword

THIS SHORT account of perhaps the most important and far-reaching success achieved by our anti-submarine forces during the whole course of the last war has been compiled with the approval of the Lords Commissioners of the Admiralty, to whom my grateful thanks are due for permission to make use of their archives.

Perhaps it is desirable to explain briefly how it came to pass that in Volume I of my official history, *The War at Sea*, it is merely stated that U.110 was sunk by British surface warships on 9th May, 1941, during the passage of Convoy OB.318, whereas now her capture is revealed. The fact is that in all the Admiralty's normal contemporary records that U-boat is shown as sunk, and no mention of her prior capture is to be found except in one small file which, doubtless for reasons of security, was kept apart from the main mass of the wartime archives. Very few people seem even to have known of the existence of this file; nor, until quite recently, did any officer or man who took part in the capture—or was aware that the U-boat had been captured—mention it to me. I have no doubt at all that, had the matter come to my notice earlier, no objection would have been raised to me telling the story in the official history, though considerations of space would have prevented it being told in full; and an amendment has already been prepared to fill the gap in the next edition of *The War at Sea*. It is, of course, an occupational hazard of the contemporary historian that he may miss some incident which he would have recounted had he known about it; and quite a number of correspondents from all over the world have in recent years actually drawn my attention to points not mentioned in my histories, but about which they possessed special knowledge. In some instances they were only of minor significance, but in several cases I have made, or shall make, additions to the history when a new edition is published. The capture of U.110 obviously comes within that category.

Two occurrences led me to seek permission to publish this book. The first was a letter from Captain A. J. Baker-Cresswell, D.S.O., R.N., telling me briefly what had happened in his Escort Group eighteen years earlier, and the second was the appearance of the book entitled *We Captured a U-boat* by Rear-Admiral D. V. Gallery, U.S.N. Captain Baker-Cresswell's letter at once drew my attention to the gap in my official history, and caused me fully to investigate the incident to which he referred; and the fruits of that research made me realise that the Royal Navy had never been given any credit for what was certainly a most important accomplishment. The more or less simultaneous study of Admiral Gallery's book next made it clear to me that certain of the claims he made for his own ship and service would not hold water, and that the whole matter of the capture of enemy submarines between 1939 and 1945 had got badly out of perspective; for it is a fact that well before Admiral Gallery towed U.505 triumphantly into Bermuda we had captured two German and three Italian submarines, and had boarded and searched several others—and had said very little about it. We British are notoriously slow and diffident about publicising our successes, and by thus hiding our light under a bushel we not uncommonly allow others to claim a disproportionate share of the credit. In the present instance I felt that we had allowed matters to go altogether too far in that direction—the more so because the capture of U.110 in 1941 (with which I am here primarily concerned) far transcended in importance the capture of U.505 by Admiral Gallery and his men just over three years later. It will thus be seen that this book owes its appearance to two independent causes—research into the full details of an operation about which I had hitherto been totally unaware, and the provocation I felt over the inaccuracy of certain claims made (doubtless unwittingly) by a representative of the Royal Navy's closest ally and greatest friend.

Every one of the principal actors in this highly dramatic encounter whom I have been able to trace has given me the benefit of his recollections, and a number of them have been kind enough to read this book in draft form. I would particularly thank Captain A. J. Baker-Cresswell, D.S.O., R.N., and Captain I. H. Bockett-Pugh, D.S.O., R.N., who have answered all my importunities with great patience, and without whose help many vital details of the operation would have been lost to posterity. I also owe a great deal to Mr. J. C. Gardner and the staff of the Admiralty's Record Office on whom I could reliably depend to find any paper I asked for— provided only that it had reached the Admiralty; and Commander M. G. Saunders of the Foreign Documents Section has helped me greatly in the essential work of com- paring German records with our own. Inevitably discrepancies arise, but in all except a very few cases—and those generally of no great moment—it has been possible to reconcile them reasonably enough to enable me to offer this book to the public in the assurance that it has been made as accurate as is humanly possible.

For permission to use the illustrations in this book I am indebted to the Imperial War Museum for No. 2 and 5, to the Admiralty for Nos. 1, 3 and 4, to Captain A. J. Baker-Cresswell, D.S.O., R.N., for Nos. 6, 7, 8 and 13, to Captain V. F. Smith, D.S.O., R.N.R., for No. 12, to Barry C. Sheen, Esq., for Nos. 10 and 11, to David E. Balme, Esq., for No. 14 and to Messrs Wright & Logan for No. 9. The maps are all based on original track charts and reports in the Admiralty's possession, which are Crown Copyright.

(*Sgd.*) S. W. ROSKILL

Blounce,
South Warnborough, 1958

CHAPTER I

Capture in Ancient and
Modern Times

EVER SINCE the earliest times fighting seamen have striven
to capture enemy vessels rather than sink them. For many
centuries the urge behind that purpose was ordinary human
greed; but it is likely that the acquisition of knowledge about
the other side's movements and intentions—what we nowadays
call Intelligence—was always an important subsidiary purpose,
if only because it might lead to further captures and so to
further material gain. Thus in the days of the first Elizabeth,
when English seamen constantly scoured the oceans with the
object of seizing the ships which carried the treasure of the
New World home to Spain, the need to discover the dates
when they would sail and the routes which they would follow
was always very much to the fore. Elizabeth I took a very
lively interest in the robbing of her Spanish cousin. The
expeditions which set out for that purpose were financed somewhat on the lines of a modern joint stock company, with the
Queen herself often putting up a considerable proportion
of the capital needed to equip them; and a successful expedi-
tion would return to its promoters a fantastically high dividend.
Small wonder that such possibilities held a strong appeal for
the adventurous and ambitious seamen of the sixteenth
century.

When regular warships came to replace the armed merchantmen of the Tudor monarchs a new financial incentive to capture

was introduced. Thus in the Second Dutch War (1665–67) a " captor's encouragement " of 10s. per ton and £6 13s. 4d. per gun of an enemy ship was introduced. Not until 1692 was Prize regulated by an Act of Parliament (4 & 5 William & Mary, cap. 25), which divided the value of a capture equally between the captors, the Treasury of the Navy (principally for relief of the sick and wounded), and the Crown. In 1708 came the famous " Cruizers Act " (6 Anne, cap. 13), which transferred the whole benefit from the Crown to the captors after condemnation of the prize in the Court of Admiralty, and that principle, though modified from time to time, was maintained until recently. The continued dominance of the financial incentive is well expressed by an Act of 1756 (29 Geo. II, cap. 34), which extended the granting of all prize money to the captors for the duration of the Seven Years' War, " for the encouragement of seamen and the most speedy and effectual manning of the Navy "; and during the Wars of American Independence (1778–83) and of the French Revolution (1793-1802) further acts of Parliament confirmed the captor's rights. Not a few great country estates of the eighteenth and nineteenth centuries owed their foundation to the good fortune of a senior naval officer in capturing valuable prizes.

In 1864, however, all previous Acts were repealed (27–28 Victoria, cap. 23), and Prize of War was redefined. The Naval Prize Fund was distributed according to that Act after both the German wars of this century, but on 19th December, 1945, it was abolished. Thus, after nearly three centuries, did the financial incentive to capture at sea finally disappear. It is curious, and perhaps significant, that this should have come to pass exactly at the time when our Governments started to pay large financial sums to persons whose technical inventions were considered to have contributed substantially to the war effort.

But the second motive behind the urge to capture an enemy

vessel, that of gaining intelligence, retained some importance even at the time when financial gain was, sometimes to an excessive extent, the primary object. Thus during the Napoleonic Wars one frequently finds British officers interrogating the crews of captured ships with the object of discovering enemy movements and intentions; and it is perhaps natural that as the pecuniary motive declined, the gaining of intelligence should have increased in importance until in the wars of this century it became dominant. To-day it is the only reason for capturing an enemy vessel; but the collection of intelligence plays such a vital part in modern war that capture has lost none of the importance which it held in the days when Elizabethan seamen wished to make " Her Majesty mistress of more treasure than any of her progenitors ever enjoyed."

The intelligence which can to-day be gained from a capture can be divided into two broad classes—technical and operational. The former includes knowledge of the construction and equipment of an enemy ship; and its acquisition can greatly improve the counter-measures adopted against others of her class and type, besides assisting our own naval architects and technicians in improving their designs. By operational intelligence we mean the acquisition of knowledge regarding the enemy's present activities and future intentions—with the purpose firstly of attacking his forces at moments of our own choosing, and secondly of avoiding engagements in circumstances where the advantage will lie with the enemy. An example of the first purpose would be the despatch of a striking force to catch an enemy surface raider at her fuelling rendezvous; while the routeing of convoys clear of waters in which U-boats are known to be lying in wait provides a good example of the second.

Several excellent examples of the immense benefits which may be derived from such captures are to be found in the annals of the 1914–18 war; and with such recent and profitable experience available to us it was natural that the Admiralty should stress the desirability of once again acquiring intelligence of that nature when, in 1939, war broke out with Germany for the second time. In particular they drew attention to the great benefits which might be derived from the capture of an enemy U-boat. British escort commanders at once took up the idea with zest; for each one of them hoped that the honour of making the first capture would fall to him. Boarding parties were formed, trained, and kept ready to leave their ship at a moment's notice; and in every counter-attack on a detected enemy the possibility of such a chance arising was kept very much in mind. But capture of a U-boat always presented particular problems and difficulties. In the first place the primary duty of the convoy escorts always was the safety of their merchant ship charges; and it is one of the strongest traditions of the Royal Navy that no purpose whatsoever can supersede that of ensuring the " safe and timely arrival " of a convoy. Thus if an enemy submarine was forced to the surface during an attack on a convoy the senior officer present was at once faced by a critical dilemma. Whilst fully conscious of the tremendous advantages to be gained by capture, he could not know how grievously his adversary was damaged. Should the U-boat have suffered only slightly she might yet escape, and the escort commander's first reaction would therefore probably be to sink her as quickly as possible, and so save the merchantmen from suffering further loss at her hands. The quickest way of accomplishing this was to ram the enemy, and there were many occasions on which this was attempted or accomplished; but such action eliminated, of course, any possibility of gaining intelligence—except that which might be obtained through the interrogation of prisoners. Although skilled interrogation could yield valuable results, and often did so, it was obviously a poor substitute for the knowledge which might be gained from the rapid search of a captured submarine. Thus we realised that although capture still remained highly important, it had to be left to the decision of the escort commanders to judge whether it could be attempted without endangering their convoys. Moreover, other factors, such as the state of the sea, critically affected the issue, and made the decision whether or not to attempt capture a matter for very nice judgement. Not only are the occasions when an escort vessel's seaboat can be safely launched in the open Atlantic comparatively rare, but a surfaced U-boat had a sufficient turn of speed—if she managed to start her diesel engines—to escape from almost all the types of escort which we had in service in the early days of the war, except the comparatively few destroyers which we could spare for service in that capacity. Another difficulty was that, whereas a small warship's plating was extremely thin, a U-boat's pressure hull was remarkably tough; and ramming could therefore cause more damage to the former than to the latter. In fact the damage, and even the disablement, of little ships which did ram U-boats became so serious that, at the time when our shortage of escorts was most acute, the Admiralty issued an order discouraging the practice of ramming except in cases of extreme urgency, where failure to do so might imperil the merchantmen. This aggravated the difficulties which beset an escort commander, since gunfire, even if it succeeded in hitting the very small target presented by a surfaced U-boat, was very unlikely to sink it. There remained, however, the possibility that by the judicious dropping of shallow-set depth charges, and the use of the escort vessel's smaller guns, the enemy's crew, whose morale and resolution might well have suffered from earlier depth charging, could be persuaded or encouraged to abandon ship; and if that could be accomplished the possibility of capturing her at once became more favourable—if only the weather permitted the working of boats.

After the Admiralty had stressed both the desirability of capture and the danger of ramming, the broad aims of our escort group commanders became, firstly, to sink any U-boat they detected by depth charge attacks while she was submerged; secondly to prevent at all costs the escape of an enemy which was forced to surface; and thirdly to lose no chance of boarding and capturing a U-boat, provided that such action would not endanger the merchantmen. This book sets out to tell how this latter purpose was accomplished by one escort group with singular success and immense benefit to the Allied cause. But before embarking on that hitherto untold story it is desirable briefly to recount other instances of submarine captures made during the war of 1939–45.

CHAPTER II

Other Submarine Captures
1939 - 1945

It actually fell to the Germans to make the first capture of a submarine during the last war. Late in April 1940 the British *Seal* left the Humber to lay mines in the Kattegat. This was bound to be an exceedingly hazardous operation, especially for a submarine as big as the *Seal*, which displaced about 2,150 tons when submerged. In fact so grave were the dangers that the Commander of her flotilla, Captain J. S. Bethell, came specially to London from his base at Blyth to urge Admiral Max Horton, who was then Flag Officer, Submarines, to reconsider his intention to send her on such a mission. The Admiral, however, who had himself worked in those waters in the 1914–18 war, though in the much smaller E-boats, adhered to his decision; and Bethell returned north feeling depressingly sure that the *Seal* would never survive her patrol. Her prospects had, moreover, recently been further reduced by the occupation of Denmark and southern Norway by the Germans; for it was now certain that those shallow waters, where a raiding submarine could not seek safety in the depths, had been heavily mined by the enemy, and would also be constantly patrolled by his surface ships and aircraft.

It soon became plain that such apprehensions were fully justified; for the *Seal* was bombed by German aircraft soon after she entered the Kattegat on 4th May; but they did little damage. Although aware that his ship's presence must now be known to the enemy, and that search and counter-attack were virtually certain, the *Seal's* Captain (Lieutenant-Commander R. P. Lonsdale) carried on with his mission, and that same morning he successfully laid his entire outfit of 50 mines. As German records reveal that two merchantmen totalling 5,488 tons, as well as two small patrol vessels, were sunk by the *Seal's* mines her sortie certainly achieved results. Hardly had Lonsdale completed his mission when he sighted a flotilla of enemy anti-submarine vessels through his periscope, and was thus left in no doubt that he was about to undergo a very dangerous hunt. The searchers were actually the German 12th Anti-submarine Flotilla, commanded by Fregatten-kapitän Hans Korn.[1] At full strength it consisted of thirteen UJ boats (U-Jägers or submarine-hunters), most of which were converted trawlers of 350–525 tons displacement; but we do not know exactly how many were present on this occasion. In the afternoon the *Seal's* Captain saw that a number of motor torpedo-boats had joined in the hunt, and as these fast vessels were more dangerous than the converted trawlers he took evasive action. In doing so he unwittingly took his ship through a German minefield.

By 6 p.m. the *Seal* had not shaken off her pursuers, and her Captain therefore made another alteration of course, dived to 70 feet and stopped all motors. Half an hour later a heavy explosion shook her most severely. The after compartments of the submarine were flooded, and she went to the bottom in about 90 feet with her bows inclined sharply upwards. Shortly before midnight, after nearly six hours of

---

[1] The following are British equivalents of the German ranks:—

> Fregattenkapitän—Commander
> Korvettenkapitän—Lieutenant-Commander
> Kapitänleutnant—Senior Lieutenant
> Oberleutnant-zur-See—Junior Lieutenant
> Leutnant-zur-See—Sub-Lieutenant

agonising struggle to repair the damage sufficiently to enable her to escape, the crew began the fight to regain the surface. At first all their efforts seemed likely to prove vain, and as a last resort they used most of the small reserve of compressed air to blow out diesel fuel and so lighten the hull. At 1 a.m. on the 5th, by which time the *Seal's* crew had almost abandoned hope of seeing daylight again, the submarine suddenly rose steeply to the surface at an angle of 30 degrees. But her predicament was indeed desperate. The electric motors were flooded, and only one diesel engine could be coaxed into moving—and that very slowly in the astern direction. As her rudder was jammed hard-a-starboard she could, moreover, only move in a circle; and the high air pressure and lack of oxygen inside the hull had reduced her crew to the point of total exhaustion. Thus her Captain's intention to make for Swedish territorial waters, though only a few miles away, could hardly have been carried out. As, moreover, dawn started to break at 3 a.m. the *Seal* would only enjoy the friendly shield of darkness for about two hours, after which renewed search and attack were certain.

Shortly after surfacing the *Seal* managed to get away a signal to the Admiralty reporting her grievous predicament; and the reply was that, after destroying all the secret material in his ship, her Captain should regard the safety of his crew as the primary consideration. That message was, however, never received in the stricken submarine, because the crew had already destroyed the wireless sets, as well as all other equipment and documents which might have been valuable to the enemy. None the less the *Seal* actually carried out the Admiralty instructions, almost to the letter.

Immediately after daylight German aircraft attacked with machine guns, and inflicted several casualties. Among the wounded was the First Lieutenant. Next a seaplane landed close to the stricken and helpless *Seal*, while the anti-submarine vessel UJ.128,[1] commanded by Kapitänleutnant Lang, came close alongside, and at 6.30 sent a boarding officer and prize crew on board. The seaplane had meanwhile taken prisoner the *Seal's* Captain and a Petty Officer. Leutnant Nolte, the boarding officer, certainly acted with initiative and promptitude, his primary aim being to prevent the submarine sinking. Having assembled the remaining officers in the control room, and kept ten of her crew aboard, he went right through the submarine as far as the water-tight door at the after end of the diesel room, abaft which she was completely flooded. Her considerable trim by the stern and list to port were meanwhile steadily increasing, and the Chief Engineer warned him that he expected her to capsize within ten minutes. " I replied," said Nolte in his report, " that we would then all sink together." He next ascertained for himself that what his British prisoners had told him was true, namely that the diesel engines, as well as the electric motors in the flooded after compartment, were completely out of action, and that very little compressed air remained. Thus there was no possibility of righting the submarine by blowing the port side ballast tanks. The list had by this time become so bad that the men inside the hull, British and Germans, had great difficulty in maintaining a foothold. Meanwhile the UJ.128 had come alongside, passed a wire and taken the *Seal* in tow.

Nolte was fully aware of the need to search for papers and material which could be of value to the German intelligence authorities, but one of the crew told him that " they had had plenty of time to destroy all secret papers," a fact which he acknowledged " to appear very probable "; for there were everywhere signs of the thoroughness with which they had carried out that duty. All instruments had been completely demolished, and the few books and papers which he collected from inside the submarine were utterly valueless. With typical German thoroughness these were carefully listed later. They

[1] This was the former trawler *Franken,* of 435 Gross Register Tons.

included nothing more interesting than the Wardroom Wine and Tobacco accounts, the Manual of Seamanship (which can be bought at any bookstall in England), a copy of the King's Regulations, that well-known aid to preparation for the examination for the rank of Lieutenant entitled " Queries in Seamanship," and the Master-at-Arms's Rough Report Book.

Nolte, who was evidently endowed with a sense of humour, plainly enjoyed his novel and exciting experience—and that in spite of the *Seal*'s crew being convinced, and trying hard to convince him, that she would sink at any moment. Thus he reported that when an officer offered him a glass of rum— " Navy rum, of particularly good quality in England "—he " had nothing against drinking a glass, which tasted excellent." When he realised that there was nothing more he could do aboard, he verified that all valves were closed and called the prisoners on deck. " The British," he reported, " were very courteous, and invited me to precede them out of the ship. But I said it was unnecessary, as I already felt quite at home." Captors and prisoners were now ferried by motor boat to the UJ.128, where the British officers were separated from their men and a preliminary interrogation took place. Beer and spirits were offered, evidently in the hope of loosening tongues; but one man who assured Nolte that " the British Home Fleet had mostly been destroyed " was evidently suspected of pulling his leg. The recent Norwegian campaign and the rescue of the *Altmark*'s prisoners by the *Cossack* were discussed in general terms; but nothing of the slightest value to the Germans was gained from this or from later interrogations. Some of the prisoners did, however, evidently talk a good deal more freely than should have been the case; and it gave Nolte (and probably his superiors as well) some satisfaction to be told that the British admired the performance of the German Navy in the Norwegian Campaign, " especially in sending an expeditionary force to Norway without possessing command of the sea."

On approaching Frederikshaven on the east coast of Denmark on the evening of the 6th May the UJ.128 turned her tow over to the salvage vessel *Seeteufel*. By that time the *Seal's* list had increased to 45 degrees, and all three after compartments were flooded. She can only have been got in by a very narrow margin. The two wounded officers had meanwhile been taken to the hospital at Arlborg, and the Commander of the German Naval Group Command East, Admiral Rolf Carls, ordered that the other prisoners (three officers and fifty-two men) should be sent to Kiel, where further interrogation was to be carried out in the presence of Dönitz's Chief of the Operations Division, Korvettenkapitän Eberhard Godt. As has been said, the enemy learnt little of value, except perhaps details of the operation on which the *Seal* had been engaged. By the 7th May the salvage authorities at Frederikshaven had got her on to an even keel; but next day she again took a heavy list to port and examination by divers revealed holes in the pressure hull. None the less by the 10th she was ready for removal to Kiel, and left in tow of three tugs. The Germans examined her very thoroughly, and the Ober Kommando Marine (O.K.M., the equivalent of the British Admiralty) ordered that she should be made seaworthy in the Germania Yard at Kiel. Their intention was to carry out trials with her, manned by a German crew; and she was commissioned into the 1st U-boat Flotilla at Kiel on the last day of November. After a short period with the 3rd U-boat Flotilla in 1941 she reverted to the Base Command at Kiel, and on 31st July was paid off. She was not actually released for breaking up until the end of October 1942. Thus the British crew involved in what must have seemed to them a tragic disaster may console themselves with the knowledge that the enemy was never able to make their ship operational. It appears that the most valuable knowledge acquired from her by the Germans came about through finding six reserve torpedoes in the submarine. Once she had been damaged it was, of course, quite impossible for the crew to fire or jettison these. The German technicians who inspected them reported that the British contact torpedo pistol " was of very good and effective design and manufacture "; and Dönitz at once recommended its introduction into his service " in order to overcome troubles with our own pistol."

In the enemy's camp there was natural jubilation at the capture of a British man-of-war, and their propaganda service quickly took full advantage of it. On our side, where the full facts could not of course be known, there was some consternation, and measures were at once introduced to make it possible to scuttle an injured submarine. So remote had the possibility of capture appeared to us that, at the time of the disaster to the *Seal*, none of our submarines was fitted with scuttling charges to enable them to sink themselves quickly in an emergency.[1] The whole truth regarding her ordeal did not become known until the prisoners were released from captivity after the war, and the German side of the story of her last patrol also became available to us. The *Seal*'s Captain and the officer who became second-in-command after the First Lieutenant was wounded were then tried by Courts Martial; but in face of the evidence which the defence was able to offer against the charges of failure to engage the enemy and of allowing the submarine to fall into enemy hands, they were both honourably acquitted. We may allow that

[1] After the loss of three submarines (the *Seahorse*, *Undine* and *Starfish*) while on patrol in the Heligoland Bight in January 1940, and the discovery that the crews of two of them had been made prisoner, the Admiralty ordered the fitting of two depth charges in the bilges of submarines which were to patrol in shallow water close off the enemy's coasts. The charges were set to explode at 50 feet depth, and the idea was that if the interior of the submarine was flooded and she sank in any depth greater than that set on the depth charge pistols, they would destroy the submarine. The *Seal* was fitted with such depth charges; but they could not, of course, be used to scuttle the ship, and as her hull never became wholly flooded they did not function at all.

great submarine commander Admiral Sir Max Horton to have the last word on the subject. Though he was certainly not an officer who would overlook any failure in a subordinate, in the case of the *Seal* he considered that, lacking all electric as well as almost all motive power, and not being fitted with scuttling charges, the self-destruction of the damaged ship was virtually impossible. Finally we may remark that even had the crew succeeded in sinking her in about 90 feet of water close off an enemy coast, she could certainly have been salvaged without undue difficulty. In view of the foregoing the justice of post-war verdicts is clear beyond question.

In 1958 the Captain of the *Seal* wrote to the author of this book a very generous letter setting out the salient facts of what he called " the most momentous days in his life." In this letter he recalled how his damaged ship went to the bottom of the Kattegat at about 6.30 p.m. on 4th May, 1941, and how he had to wait until it became dark at about 11 p.m. before trying to bring her to the surface again. As the next day would begin to break at 3 a.m. he knew that he had not more than four hours of night time in which to make good his escape. " For the next $2\frac{1}{2}$ hours," he wrote, " we tried everything that I or anyone else could think of to get to the surface, but without success. At 1.30 a.m. I therefore called the whole crew into the Control Room to say prayers before we made one final attempt. We had no new ideas to try, and I myself could not see any reason why we should be more successful than before; but in the back of my mind was the thought, ' with God all things are possible.' Then, after I had said prayers, a new idea came to me. We were lying with our bows inclined 30 degrees upwards, and it occurred to me that if I could get more weight at the forward end without adding to our total weight it might succeed in breaking our stern out of the muddy bottom. We therefore rigged a handline from the torpedo compartment to the control room, and all men who could be spared from other duties hauled themselves right forward along the line. Then we made our final effort and, as you know, at once came to the surface. Our small Faith had been answered in a way that, to many of us seemed miraculous. When we opened the conning tower hatch we found our bows were pointing directly towards the Danish coast, which had just been occupied by the Germans. I did all I could to turn her towards Gothenburg in Sweden, which I hoped to reach; but she obstinately refused to point in any direction except Denmark. It was my Coxswain, Joe Higgins, who jocularly suggested that we might get to Sweden stern first. Higgins was one of the finest men who ever lived—always cheerful and efficient, and his spirit rose above every difficulty. During the next five years in prisoner-of-war camps his example of moral courage and cheerfulness was worth more to those around him than man can measure. He was a humble man, but a very great one. When last I heard from him he was working for Gamages.

" I do not expect," Lonsdale continued in his letter, " ever to forget the shock which I experienced a few days after my capture when out for a walk under guard at Kiel, I saw the *Seal* being towed into port; nor, almost worse, when on leaving Kiel for the prison camp I caught sight of her in dry dock. Later on we read reports in German papers about how she was helping our enemies; and it was indeed an immense relief to find out after the war that those reports were not true. . . . Looking back it is, of course, obvious that apart from what we did to minimise the consequences of the disaster, the one additional measure necessary was for me to stay behind and *see* that she was sunk by one or other of the measures we might have tried." Even if true, that re-appraisal of his actions takes no account of the effects of the tremendous ordeal through which he and his men had just passed.[1]

Two months after the *Seal* was captured another British

---

[1] In 1948 Commander Lonsdale was ordained Priest in the Church of England.

submarine underwent a somewhat similar ordeal while on patrol in the Skagerrak. The *Shark* (Lieutenant-Commander P. N. Buckley) was a much smaller vessel than the *Seal*, and displaced only 960 tons when submerged. But at that time of year in those latitudes there was practically no darkness, and soon after Buckley had surfaced to charge batteries at about 10 p.m. on 5th July he was attacked by German aircraft while in the act of diving, and suffered such severe damage that he had to resurface. The *Shark*'s crew, who could not use their 3-inch gun because of the structural damage, then fought the attackers with their smaller weapons, and shot down one aircraft. But they themselves suffered heavy casualties from machine-gun fire, and after running out of ammunition they could only await the arrival of surface craft. Next morning two German minesweeping trawlers arrived, took off the wounded and the survivors, and then tried to take the *Shark* in tow. Although the last man to leave the stricken submarine had opened her ballast tanks to the sea, she did not sink until the towing trawler went ahead. Probably her hydroplanes (vertical rudders) were angled to force her downwards. The Germans thus gained nothing of any value; but the loss of the *Shark* did emphasise the grave danger of sending submarines into those waters during the summer months.

Little more than a month after the disaster to the *Seal*, to be precise on 19th June, 1940, the Italian submarine *Galileo Galilei* was captured in the Red Sea, and brought into Aden. Three days previously she had sunk a Norwegian tanker, the *James Stove*, and then used her guns to stop a Yugoslav freighter, whom she subsequently released. The gunfire was reported by coast-watchers, and Gladiator fighters of No. 94 Squadron of the R.A.F. were sent out to investigate its source.

On the 18th a Gladiator sighted the *Galilei* about 30 miles south-east of Aden, and shadowed her until a Blenheim bomber arrived. The submarine was then on the surface charging her batteries; but she dived as the Blenheim attacked, and neither the bombs nor the Gladiator's machine-gun fire did her appreciable damage. Meanwhile the destroyer *Kandahar* and the sloop *Shoreham* had been sent out from Aden hot foot, to reinforce the search by several patrol vessels which were already in the vicinity. The *Kandahar*, under Commander W. G. A. Robson[1], was one of the four modern destroyers sent through the Suez Canal from the Mediterranean when Italy's attitude became threatening; while the *Shoreham*, under Lieutenant-Commander F. D. Miller, belonged to the Red Sea Escort Force which then formed part of Vice-Admiral Sir Ralph Leatham's East Indies Command.

After dark on the 18th the hunted Italian submarine surfaced, and was rash enough to use her wireless. The *Kandahar* picked up her transmission and led the search in the right direction. It was the *Shoreham*, however, who gained the first contact; but the submarine dived at 7.30 p.m. and successfully evaded two attacks. The larger British ships, believing the enemy to have been damaged, now withdrew, leaving the small trawler *Moonstone*, whose skipper was Bosun W. J. H. Moorman, on patrol. Moorman had entered the Navy in 1921 from the Greenwich Royal Hospital School at the age of 15½, and was promoted to Warrant Officer in 1936. The trawler was his first command, and when he commissioned her at Malta shortly before the outbreak of war he could hardly have imagined that it would fall to his lot to achieve the first capture of an enemy submarine. When he received orders to hurry off to sea on the evening of the 18th half his crew were ashore on leave. They were at once recalled, and three of them, including the gunlayer of the only 4-inch

---

[1] Now Admiral Sir Geoffrey Robson, K.B.E., C.B., D.S.O., D.S.C. He served with great distinction in destroyers, and was twice sunk during the war. The *Kandahar* was lost after striking a mine off Tripoli on 19th December, 1941, and the *Hardy*, also under Robson, fell victim to a U-boat's torpedo on 30th January, 1944, while escorting convoy JW.56B to Murmansk.

gun, actually scrambled aboard from a private motor boat as she was leaving harbour. It would have been difficult for the trawler to fight an action without those three men.

In the early hours of the 19th the *Galilei* surfaced for a short time, probably to refresh the air inside her hull; but at 2.30 a.m. she submerged again. Blenheims of No. 203 Squadron searched a wide area of sea at dawn, but in the overcast monsoon weather then prevailing they failed to resight the quarry. Not until 11.37 a.m., when the *Moonstone* obtained an Asdic contact at long range, was any further sign of her presence obtained. Because the little trawler could only make headway slowly in the heavy sea then running, she could not fire a full pattern of depth charges without grave risk of injuring herself. Moorman therefore dropped only one charge, set to explode at 150 feet; but the submarine had probably heard her approach, and had gone deep. Nearly an hour later the trawler regained contact at only 300 yards range, and quickly dropped another charge, followed by a second one. A few minutes later the *Galilei* came to the surface about a mile astern of the trawler, and opened fire on her tormentor with machine guns. The *Moonstone* promptly reversed her course, and returned the enemy's fire to such good effect that the Italians were prevented from manning their two 3.9-inch guns. Then, closing to 500 yards, the trawler swept the submarine's decks with a hail of machine-gun bullets, and scored several hits on her conning tower with 4-inch shells. One of these latter killed the *Galilei*'s captain (Capitano di Corvetta Corrado Nardi) and, according to eye-witnesses in the *Moonstone*, produced something like panic among her crew who rushed on deck, hauled down their colours and waved white clothing as a further sign of surrender. At 12.25 the *Moonstone* accordingly ceased fire, and closed her adversary with the intention of taking possession of the prize; but her boat had been damaged by bullets, and Moorman therefore decided to await the arrival of reinforcements. Next another aircraft came on the scene, and, not realising that the *Galilei* had surrendered, dropped two bombs and fired her machine guns. Luckily no damage was done. At 1.34 p.m. the *Kandahar* arrived, sent a prize crew on board the submarine and took her in tow. The rough sea, however, made towing very difficult, and the wire soon parted; but the engineers in the prize crew got the captive's main engines running, and she actually arrived in Aden, with the White Ensign flying above the Italian flag, under her own power. British records show that the *Galilei* lost thirteen of her crew by gunfire or drowning, and had four more wounded; three officers and 37 ratings from her landed at Aden as prisoners. The Italian naval historian on the other hand states that she was " found drifting aimlessly after almost all of her officers and crew had been killed in the attack, and her surviving crew members had become totally incapacitated by gas poisoning " (from the refrigeration plant)[1] —a version of these events which receives little support from a large number of reliable eye witnesses.

The prize was a very valuable one, and from her we obtained intelligence regarding the disposition of other Italian submarines in the Red Sea and Indian Ocean. As a result we caught and sank the *Torricelli* on the 22nd June, and the *Galvani*, which was patrolling in the Persian Gulf to catch our tanker traffic, on the following day. For his part in the capture of the *Galilei* Mr. Moorman and his Second-in-Command, Midshipman M. J. Hunter, R.N.R., were both decorated with the D.S.C., and Moorman was specially selected to take courses for promotion to commissioned rank. He retired as a Lieutenant-Commander in 1950.

In December 1940, the *Galilei* was brought up the Red Sea by a British crew, and passed through the Suez Canal to Alexandria, where her hull and equipment were very thoroughly

[1] See *Che Ha Fatto La Marina?* by Commander M. A. Bragadin (Milan, 2nd Ed., 1950), p. 42, and *The Italian Navy in World War II* by the same author (United States Naval Institute, 1957), p. 23.

inspected. Known at different times as the X.2 and P.711 in British service, the only operational use we made of her was for anti-submarine training. She remained at Alexandria until sold for scrap after the end of the war.

The next capture took place in the North Atlantic on 9th May, 1941, thousands of miles away from the scene of the *Galilei*'s surrender; and it is with that story that this book is principally concerned. At almost exactly the date when we captured U.110, a new 770-ton Type VII C. Atlantic boat numbered U.570 started her first and only commission under Korvettenkapitän Hans Rahmlow. After completing her trials at Horten in Oslo fiord she left for Trondheim on 20th July; but on her way she damaged herself slightly in a crash dive on to a rocky bottom, made to avoid attack by British aircraft. After docking for repairs she left Trondheim on 24th August. Her orders were to operate to the south of Iceland for a month, and then proceed to La Pallice in western France. Rahmlow passed to the north of the Faeroes, mostly on the surface, and reached his operational area undetected. Soon after he had arrived on patrol U-boat headquarters signalled to U.570 and about a dozen other boats to attack a convoy which was already being shadowed. There were in fact three homeward convoys, all fairly close together, in the eastern half of the north Atlantic at the time, and it is impossible to say for certain which of them the enemy intended to attack. The probability is that it was the fast Halifax convoy HX.145; but the preceding convoy of that series, HX.144, was only about 300 miles ahead of it, while the slow convoy SC.40 from Sydney (Cape Breton Island) was about midway between the two fast convoys. The ever-watchful Submarine Tracking Room in the Admiralty had, however, sensed the danger; and diversions were ordered to keep the convoys out of harm's way. It is now plain that they all passed well to the south of the U-boat patrol line established by the enemy. No losses were suffered by any of them.

Rahmlow's crew was inexperienced, and many of his men suffered constantly from sea-sickness. Nor had U.570 achieved a satisfactory standard of fighting efficiency. Moreover in submarine warfare the margin between success and disaster is often extremely narrow, and at moments of crisis everything depends on the calmness, experience and determination of the Captain, and on the confidence which the crew feel in him. Events were to show that in none of these respects was Rahmlow's leadership up to the high standard achieved by most U-boat Captains.

Early on 27th August Rahmlow dived to 90 feet in order to gain some respite for his crew, who were not enjoying the heavy seas then running. He was at the time in 62° 15′ North, 18° 35′ West—some 80 miles south of Iceland. Two hours later (to be precise at 10.50 a.m.) he came to the surface again, and at a most unlucky moment; for Hudson " S " of No. 269 Squadron of Coastal Command (Squadron-Leader J. H. Thompson, R.A.F.) which was flying an anti-submarine patrol from Kaldadarnes airfield in Iceland, was passing exactly overhead. Rahmlow had to act promptly, and he tried to crash dive; but Thompson was too quick for him. Diving from 500 feet almost to the surface of the sea he dropped four 250-pound depth charges, which exactly straddled the target. They were set to explode at only 50 feet, and the detonations smothered the U-boat in spray and shook her savagely. Inside the boat instruments were smashed and all was thrown into confusion. A certain amount of sea water entered, thus producing fear of that submariner's nightmare—chlorine gas from the batteries. Rahmlow was convinced—probably too easily—that all was lost, and ordered the crew to put on life jackets and assemble in the conning tower.

When the plumes and spray from the depth charge explosions subsided the Hudson's crew saw U.570 still on the surface, and slightly down by the bows. Men were coming out of the conning tower, and to prevent them manning their guns Thompson opened fire. The Germans then sought shelter in the conning tower, to reappear a few minutes later showing, firstly, a white flag, and then a large white-painted board. Their intention was obvious—but it was scarcely within the capabilities of the Hudson to take possession of her prize. Thompson therefore reported what had happened to his base, and continued to circle the U-boat watchfully, ready to attack again if she made an attempt to escape. In the afternoon Catalina J. of No. 209 Squadron (Flying Officer E. A. Jewiss) which had flown from Lough Erne in Northern Ireland, relieved Thompson's Hudson, and the vigil continued.

The nearest anti-submarine vessels had meanwhile been ordered to close the position at full speed; but none was very close, and the Catalina was therefore told that, if no ship had arrived by nightfall she was to warn the crew and then sink the U-boat. Luckily a trawler, the *Northern Chief* (Lieutenant N. L. Knight, R.N.R.) arrived at 10.50 p.m.; but the sea was too rough to enable her to launch a boat. The U-boat's crew must have passed a wretched day, huddled in the conning tower; but some of her officers did brave the dangers of chlorine gas and go below to destroy all confidential material. They also sent a signal to U-boat headquarters, reporting that they had been captured, and then damaged a good many instruments with hammers. Had a surface ship been able to arrive earlier it is likely that we would have captured the U-boat entirely intact, with great gain to our intelligence authorities; but that was not to be. To discourage her crew from scuttling, the *Northern Chief* next signalled that if they did so they would not be picked up. In November 1939 the Admiralty had approved the passing of orders of that nature, to discourage intercepted enemy merchantmen from sinking themselves; but they had added the proviso that the enemy crews were in fact always to be rescued.[1] There is no

[1] See Roskill *The War at Sea*, Vol. I, p. 150 (H.M.S.O. 1954).

doubt at all that the survivors of U.570 would have been treated in the same manner, even had they scuttled; but the threat seems to have had the desired effect, for she replied, rather pathetically, to the *Northern Chief*'s signal saying, " I cannot scuttle or abandon. Save us to-morrow please."

At 3.30 a.m. next morning (28th August) another trawler, the *Kingston Agate* (Lieutenant H. O. Lestrange, R.N.R.), which was fitted for towing, arrived; and she was soon followed by the destroyer *Burwell* (formerly the *Laub*, one of the old American ships transferred to Britain under the " destroyers for bases " deal), two more trawlers (the *Wastwater* and *Windermere*), and the Canadian destroyer *Niagara*. Another aircraft (manned by a Norwegian crew) also appeared and, apparently not having heard the news that U.570 had surrendered, dropped two depth charges. Luckily they did no damage. Soon after daylight the *Burwell* and the " *Lake* " class trawlers tried to take the U-boat in tow; but they were not suited to, or properly equipped for such a task—certainly not in the heavy sea then running. At about noon the First Lieutenant of the *Kingston Agate* (Temporary Lieutenant H. B. Campbell, R.N.V.R.) suggested that he might get aboard the U-boat by floating down to her on a Carley life-saving raft. His Captain at once accepted the proposal, and two of his crew volunteered to go with the First Lieutenant on what was bound to be a difficult and hazardous exploit. A line was therefore shot across to the U-boat, and very soon the three men were making the crossing. As an eye witness later described it, " One minute they were in sight of us lining the deck (of the trawler) and the next they were hidden by the towering seas." Campbell and his men got aboard the U-boat safely, forced the crew to lend them a hand, hauled across a tow rope from the *Kingston Agate*, and successfully secured it to the stern of the prize—in spite of being nearly swept overboard as they crawled aft along the submarine's narrow deck. Altogether they were on board her for about five hours, and Lieutenant Campbell was the last to leave her—after all the Germans had been safely transhipped to the *Kingston Agate*. He had carried out a remarkably fine feat of seamanship in very difficult conditions.

The trawler now took the U-boat in tow stern first; but her troubles were by no means yet over, for the tow line parted several times. Finally the *Northern Chief* took over the tow from the *Kingston Agate*, who returned to Iceland at full speed with the prisoners. U.570 was successfully beached at Thorlakshafn in Iceland late on the 29th. The initial inspections were made by experienced British submarine officers, who found that U.570 had in fact suffered very little damage. Main engines and motors, pumps and auxiliary machinery were all in working order, little water had entered the hull, and danger from chlorine gas must have been imagined by her German crew. On 5th September she was towed off the beach, and taken round to Hvalfiord. Exactly a fortnight later she was declared seaworthy. She left Hvalfiord re-christened as H.M.S. *Graph*, under Lieutenant G. R. Colvin on 29th September and reached Barrow-in-Furness on 3rd October. After refitting there in the Vickers yard she carried out very extensive trials from the Clyde, and from those trials we gained information of inestimable value to our own anti-submarine forces; for we now knew exactly what we had to contend with in the case of the most popular type of Atlantic U-boat. No less than 659 of the 869 boats commissioned by the Germans in the second world war were of the same type as U.570.

Meanwhile Rahmlow and his crew were being passed through the British interrogation routine, to whose efficiency the enemy has paid tribute since the war,[1] and we thereby gained valuable knowledge regarding other U-boats, and their equipment and methods of operating.

[1] See for example Burt and Leasor *The One That Got Away* (Collins with Michael Joseph, 1956). The authors are, however, wrong to state (p. 72, fn.1) that Leutnant Bernhard Berndt, who was later

At the end of September 1942 the Admiralty decided that the *Graph* should join our own operational submarine fleet, and commissioned her under Lieutenant P. B. Marriott. She was the only captured submarine which ever rendered such services to her captors. We cannot here follow her career under the White Ensign in detail, but an incident in which she was involved on 21st October, 1942, while patrolling against blockade runners in the Bay of Biscay, must be mentioned—if only for the sake of historical accuracy. At about 3.40 p.m. she heard propeller noises at long range, and closed in their direction; but for a long time Lieutenant Marriott could see nothing through his periscope, because of the heavy swell that was running. Just before 5 p.m., however, he gained a fleeting but clear glimpse of a conning tower. He turned at once to an attacking course, and fired four torpedoes at what he described as a " sister ship." He then altered course right round with the intention of taking a stern shot, and in doing so twice more sighted his enemy. Between 5 and 6 minutes after firing the salvo from the bow tubes, which was about the correct running time for the torpedoes to reach the target, Marriott heard two loud explosions, which were followed by a large number of lesser cracks and bangs. The *Graph*'s crew were confident that they had sunk the enemy; and as it was dark when they surfaced at 8.30 their confidence was not shaken by the fact that they sighted neither oil nor wreckage. The Admiralty—cautious as ever about accepting such claims— assessed the result as " probably sunk "; but we now know from German records that, although the *Graph* did actually attack a genuine " sister ship," namely U.333 (Cremer) she did not sink her. It therefore seems regrettable that, in a book published as late as 1958 which purports to describe her career

hounded to his death while in prison-camp by his compatriots, was captain of the captured U-boat. Rahmlow was the Captain, and Berndt his First Lieutenant.

in British hands, the author should have stated that her attack on 21st October, 1942, was successful.[1]

In December 1942 we find the *Graph* among the submarines watching Altenfiord in north Norway, where a powerful German squadron, including the giant *Tirpitz*, had been concentrated to threaten our Arctic convoys. During the latter part of 1943 the *Graph* underwent an extensive refit in Chatham dockyard, but defects again developed early in the following year, and in February 1944 she reduced to reserve at Aberdeen. The Admiralty then abandoned all intention of using her again, and in March she was towed away to be scrapped. While on passage, however, the tow parted, and she was wrecked on the island of Islay off the west coast of Scotland on 20th March; but by that time she had given the Royal Navy all the useful service of which she was capable.

The next two submarines to be captured were both Italian, and were both seized by boarding parties from British escort vessels in the Mediterranean. At 5.30 p.m. on the evening of 9th July, 1942, a look-out in the corvette *Hyacinth* (Lieutenant J. I. Jones, R.N.R.), which was on passage from Haifa to Beirut, sighted two torpedoes approaching from the port beam. She at once altered course to comb the tracks, and the torpedoes passed a few yards astern of her. The Asdic operator quickly gained contact at 1,000 yards, and Jones attacked with six depth charges set to 100–150 feet. Patches of oil came to the surface, but Jones, who was evidently experienced in anti-submarine warfare, " viewed this with scant enthusiasm," and made two more attacks with a total of eight more depth charges. At 5.45 just after the third attack, the submarine broke surface, and the *Hyacinth* engaged with all her guns. Very soon the submarine's crew could be seen abandoning ship, and when a white flag was waved the corvette ceased fire and lowered a boat with a boarding party under Lieutenant J. Pollard, R.N.R. Included in its crew was a Maltese officers'

[1] See John Drummond *H.M. U-Boat* (W. H. Allen, 1958).

cook named John Zammit, who was to act as interpreter. Sub-Lieutenant J. Rowley, R.N.V.R., and Able Seaman Sharratt of the boarding party were the first to leap on to the submarine's deck, and they forced those of the crew who were still on board, who included all the officers, back into the conning tower. The *Hyacinth* was meanwhile picking up those who had taken to the water. They were at once placed in the fo'c's'le head under guard, and a preliminary interrogation took place, with another Maltese rating, Officers' Steward Simmons, acting as interpreter.

Pollard had meanwhile inspected the inside of the submarine, which turned out to be the *Perla*, and when he reported that she was fit for towing Jones signalled to Haifa for assistance. The corvette *Gloxinia* and two M.T.B.s at once put out to sea, while a Fleet Air Arm Walrus amphibian took off to provide air anti-submarine escort. Two submarine experts, Commander H. C. Browne and Commander (E) W. G. Pulvertaft, came out from the base, and one of the M.T.B.s rushed them onboard the captured vessel, where they took charge of the remainder of the Italian crew, who co-operated very willingly in restarting machinery and making the *Perla* seaworthy. By 10 p.m. she had been taken in tow by the *Hyacinth* and was heading for Beirut with the *Gloxinia* and M.T.B.s screening the tow. The fact that the *Perla*'s rudder was jammed hard-a-starboard caused trouble at first, and the tow parted once; but the boarding party very soon centred the rudder and thereafter no serious difficulties arose. At 1 a.m. on the 10th, only about seven hours after she had surfaced, the *Hyacinth* reached the Haifa boom, where a tug took over her prize. It had been a remarkably smart piece of work, and the men who carried it out certainly deserved the decorations awarded to them. Jones added the D.S.O. to the D.S.C. which he had gained earlier in the war, Pollard and Rowley both received D.S.C.s, and five of the *Hyacinth*'s crew were awarded the Distinguished Service Medal.

The *Perla* was a valuable prize, the more so because the boarding party had acted so quickly that her crew had no time to destroy books and documents and damage equipment. She had originally been based at Massawa in Eritrea, and her Captain (Teniente B. Napp) had got her away shortly before we captured that base on 8th April, 1941. She then sailed south, passed round the Cape of Good Hope and, after fuelling twice from German supply ships, reached Bordeaux safely on about 1st June. Her crew must be given full credit for this enterprising break-out from the Red Sea, which had become a trap for the Italian ships based there, and for taking their ship some 11,000 miles—in spite of the fact that she had not had damage from an earlier bombing attack properly repaired. The journey lasted 81 days. After being refitted by the Germans at Bordeaux she sailed south again on 15th September, passed through the Straits of Gibraltar safely in spite of being attacked by our destroyers, and reached Naples. She had sailed from Messina on her final patrol under a new Captain (Teniente G. Ventura), with five officers and 39 men, only ten days before her capture. The interrogation of the survivors yielded conflicting evidence regarding which of the *Hyacinth*'s attacks forced her to the surface; but the main weight of opinion indicated that all three did some damage—and especially the first and third. The quick arrival of Commanders Browne and Pulvertaft on board the prize undoubtedly contributed greatly to bringing her into port intact; and they commented in their report on the splendid work of Zammit as interpreter. " He gave," they said, " of his very best. His pride in Malta and his contempt for the Italians produced many delightful moments." Admiral Sir Andrew Cunningham, the Commander-in-Chief, Mediterranean, forwarded the captor's reports with the remark that the *Hyacinth* had carried out " a series of excellent attacks which allowed the *Perla* no respite "; and the Naval Staff read what they called Jones's " lively account of a very fine performance . . . with admiration." A few days after her capture the *Perla* was commissioned into the 1st Submarine Flotilla with a British crew.

Just over a year later another Italian submarine, the *Bronzo*, fell into our hands. On the 12th of July, 1943, the mine-sweepers *Cromarty* (Lieutenant-Commander C. G. Palmer, R.N.Z.N.V.R., senior officer), *Seaham*, *Poole* and *Boston* were screening the bombarding ships between Augusta and Syracuse during the combined operations for the invasion of Sicily. At 12.50 p.m. the *Seaham* (Lieutenant-Commander Robert E. Brett, R.N.R.) sighted a submarine on the surface about a mile away. Brett went full speed ahead with the intention of ramming, but when the submarine crash-dived he quickly had his depth charge settings adjusted for a shallow attack. Before he could carry it out, however, the submarine broke surface again; so Brett altered once more on to a ramming course, opened fire with his 3-inch gun, and swept the sub-marine's deck with his lighter weapons. The *Poole* and *Boston* also joined in the gun action which, however, lasted only a few minutes, as some of the crew jumped overboard while others made obvious signs of surrender. The *Seaham* quickly got a boarding party away, and the *Bronzo* was soon taken in tow. Nine of her crew had been killed, including the Captain (Teniente A. Gherardi); but 36 men were picked up and made prisoner. At 4.30 p.m., only some four hours after she was first sighted, the *Bronzo* was towed triumphantly into Syracuse. Her mission had been to attack the bombarding ships which the *Cromarty* and her consorts were protecting, and she had left the base of Pozzuoli near Naples only two days earlier.

We now come to the capture of U.505 commanded by Oberleutnant Harald Lange, by the American escort carrier *Guadalcanal* and the four destroyers who were working with her, on 4th June, 1944, off Cape Blanc in West Africa; but as Rear-Admiral Daniel V. Gallery has told that story very fully and vividly in his book *We Captured a U-boat*[1] there is no need

[1] Sidgwick and Jackson, 1957.

to recapitulate it here. But certain statements made in that account demand comment. Firstly no British officer who fought in the Atlantic Battle or in the Mediterranean will accept Admiral Gallery's implication that the idea of capturing a surfaced submarine was an original inspiration on his part; for we have already seen how many, if not most British escort commanders had such an object very much in mind from the early days of the war. Secondly, although it is true that, as Admiral Gallery points out, the case of U.570 differs from his accomplishment in capturing and bringing in U.505 in that the former was not boarded until some time after she had voluntarily surrendered to Squadron Leader Thompson's Hudson, he is wrong to claim that U.505 "was the only German submarine boarded and captured at sea" (p. 67). The facts are that, although U.570's crew had time to destroy virtually all the material which might have furnished us with valuable operational intelligence, from U.110 the gain to the Allies was every bit as great as from Gallery's U.505, and it came to us moreover at a far more critical period of the war. One can only presume that, when he wrote his book Admiral Gallery had never heard of the Royal Navy's achievement. Nor is that surprising, for the secret was so closely guarded at the time that no one except the actual participants and a few highly placed officers in the Admiralty ever knew the whole story; and although, when co-operation between the Royal and the United States Navies became complete shortly before America entered the war, we certainly passed to our Ally all the benefits gained from the capture, we seem never to have told the Americans exactly how it came to pass. It is indeed a remarkable fact that although the crews of three escort vessels, and many survivors of recently sunk merchantmen who were on board them at the time—totalling at least 400 officers and men—all knew that a U-boat had been captured, not one of them ever breathed a word about it. Rarely can discretion have been more severely tested, or a secret better kept.

But there is another very important fact regarding the capture of U.110, and moreover one which makes the accomplishment absolutely unique. Whereas the original crews of Admiral Gallery's U.505, and also of the *Galileo Galilei*, U.570, the *Perla* and the *Bronzo*, were all fully aware that their ships had been captured, so skilfully was the seizure of U.110 carried out that to this day the German survivors have never discovered that their ship fell into our hands. It will be plain to anyone versed in intelligence work that this astonishing accomplishment greatly enhanced the value of the capture; for as soon as any belligerent knows, or even suspects, that one of his ships has fallen into the other side's hands he will at once take every possible step to mitigate, if not eliminate, the harm which may have been done to his cause. But if, on the other hand, a ship is captured with her equipment intact and the enemy never discovers it, then we will be able to reap the greatest possible benefit. That was, very precisely, what happened with U.110—more than three years before Gallery's men hoisted the Stars and Stripes above the Nazi's crooked cross on board U.505 !

Lastly, to drive a final nail into the coffin in which some of the claims made with regard to U.505 should be encased, we may mention several other instances in which U-boats were boarded at sea, but their captors did not succeed in towing them in. On 10th September, 1941, while escorting convoy SC.42, the Royal Canadian Navy's newly-commissioned corvettes *Chambly* and *Moose Jaw* forced U.501 to the surface, and a boarding party from the former got aboard her and did their utmost, though unavailingly, to prevent her sinking.[1] Secondly, on 6th March, 1944, the Canadian and British ships escorting convoy HX.280 hunted U.744 for over 30 hours, and when she surfaced a boarding party from the R.C.N. corvette *Chilliwack* got on board in time not only to hoist the White Ensign but to remove what the Canadian historian

[1] See Schull *The Far Distant Ships* (Ottawa, 1952, pp. 83-86).

calls " a precious haul of books and equipment."[1] But towing was quite impossible in the heavy sea then running, and one of our own ships finally sent the U-boat to the bottom with a torpedo. Yet another example of a surfaced U-boat being boarded at sea occurred on the evening of 12th April, 1945, when the frigate *Loch Glendhu* of the Eighth Escort Group blew U.1024 to the surface in the Irish Sea, about twenty miles south of the Isle of Man. Her consorts the *Loch Achray* and *Loch More* then joined in, boarding parties were sent away and the *Loch More* took the U-boat in tow. Unhappily thick fog came down at that moment, which made towing extremely difficult. At midnight the tow parted, and the U-boat sank.

To conclude this brief survey of submarine captures, it should be recorded that, to the best of my knowledge, no Japanese or American submarine was ever captured intact by the other side during the last war. Perhaps the nearest we came to achieving such a success was when the New Zealand Navy's little minesweepers *Kiwi* and *Moa* blew the I-1 to the surface off Guadalcanal in the Solomon Islands on the night of 29th–30th January, 1943, and then fought their much larger adversary so effectively that they drove her ashore. Divers later penetrated inside the hull, from which some equipment was removed. On the American side the only time the enemy gained a glimpse of the interior of one of their submarines was when, on 23rd October, 1944, during the Battle of Leyte Gulf, the *Darter* ran ashore. The crew was taken off by another submarine, but every attempt to destroy the vessel failed, and the Japanese later boarded and inspected her. They found, however, nothing of value.

[1] *Ibid* pp. 218-223.

CHAPTER III

The Atlantic Battle, 1941

IN THE late spring and early summer of 1941 it was plain to the British authorities that events in the Atlantic were moving towards a crisis. Though the Germans had not yet decided to place U-boat construction at the top of their list of priorities, we were aware that their rate of production was increasing far more rapidly than in 1940, and that we were not sinking them nearly as fast as new boats were taking the water. In fact between 1st January and 1st April, 1941, thirty new boats were commissioned, compared with twenty-two in the previous quarter, and the enemy's total strength rose from 89 to 113. Furthermore the U-boats and long-range bombers were beginning to make full use of the bases in western France which they had acquired in June, 1940, and this greatly shortened the distance to the Atlantic convoy routes and so increased the time which each boat could spend on patrol. It was not surprising that our shipping losses in the north Atlantic should have risen from 42 ships (214,382 tons) in January to 69 ships (317,378 tons) in February, and to 63 ships (364,689 tons) in March; and the proportion of these losses caused by the U-boats was also rising steeply. With 195 ships of 687,901 tons sunk by all types of enemy action in April our losses reached the highest point so far touched during the war—not even excepting the very heavy casualties sustained during the withdrawal from Europe in June, 1940. Small wonder that the Admiralty was anxious !

But if the situation during that second spring of the war looked grave, the auguries for the not too distant future were by no means all unfavourable to the British cause. In the first place, by the occupation of Iceland in May, 1940, we had to some extent offset the advantage the enemy had gained by the invasion of Norway. It was true that the invisible barrier of British sea power, through which commerce raiders had to break, had been forced back from the historic line between the Shetland Islands and Norway to the middle of the Atlantic, which made it far easier for the enemy's surface and underwater craft to evade our sea and air patrols; but the possession of bases in Iceland enabled our Atlantic escorts to extend their protection much farther out into the ocean. Instead of having to leave the convoys with sufficient fuel to return to bases in Northern Ireland, they could now carry on to a point south of Iceland, and then steam the much shorter distance to one of its harbours to replenish; and it was possible for other escorts based on Iceland to come south to meet the convoys, and take over their protection from the ships which had started out from Britain. These measures enabled us to extend the protecting shield of the convoy escorts from about 19° West, which was the farthest point to which they had been able to reach at the end of 1940, to about 35° West, which was half-way across the northern ocean. Nor was the extension of surface escort the only benefit derived from the occupation of Iceland; for it also enabled the Royal Air Force to establish bases there, and so extend the range of Coastal Command's shore-based aircraft much farther out into the ocean. By 1941 we fully realised the vital importance of air escort in the struggle against the U-boats, and were making every endeavour to strengthen No. 15 Group of Coastal Command, which was responsible for the North Atlantic. In April of that year the Air Ministry established a separate wing (No. 30) in Iceland under the control of No. 15 Group, and in the same month the Admiralty assumed operational control of all Coastal Command aircraft. These measures greatly strengthened our sea-air co-operation, and by sending our

Atlantic convoys by northerly routes they were able to gain the maximum protection from the Iceland-based aircraft.

By the spring of 1941 we had also got over the first shock of the " wolf pack " tactics introduced by the Germans in the previous autumn, when their night attacks on the surface had found a weak spot in our defensive organisation and training; and early in the following year we had dealt the U-boat command a heavy blow by depriving it of three of its most famous " aces." The death of Prien, who had penetrated into Scapa and sunk the *Royal Oak* on 14th October, 1939, in U.47 and of Schepke in U.100, and the capture of Kretschmer from U.99, all of which took place within a few days in March, 1941, were more important accomplishments than we could possibly have realised at the time.[1] Other developments favourable to our cause owed an enormous debt to the vision and drive of Admiral Sir Percy Noble, who had taken over the Western Approaches command when its headquarters were shifted from Plymouth to Liverpool in February, 1941; for it was he who introduced permanent escort groups, who organised thorough training in anti-submarine tactics, who standardised our practices and procedure, and also achieved the intimate collaboration between the Western Approaches escorts and the aircraft of Coastal Command's No. 15 Group, which was to yield such decisive results at the crisis of the battle in May, 1943. From the very beginning Air Vice-Marshal

[1] For an account of the sinking of U.99 and U.100 by the destroyers *Walker* and *Vanoc* on 17th March, 1941, see Captain Donald Macintyre *U-boat Killer* (Weidenfeld and Nicolson, 1956). According to post-war statistics prepared in Germany (see *Marine Rundschau* for October 1957) Kretschmer's successes place him first on the list of outstanding U-boat commanders with 44 ships totalling 266,629 tons sunk while in command of U.23 and U.99. Prien's name stands 10th on the same list with 28 ships totalling 160,935 tons sunk by U.47, and Schepke is 11th with 39 ships of 159,130 tons to his credit while in command of U.3, U.19 and U.100.

Robb, commander of No. 15 Group, established himself in the next door room to Admiral Noble in the Western Approaches Command headquarters in Derby House, Liverpool; and the close contact between the sea and air forces engaged in the Atlantic battle thereby established was of immense benefit to the Allied cause.

Once the permanent escort groups, two of which played the leading parts in our story, had been formed, we made every endeavour not to break them up. The reason was that a close understanding between individual Captains was found to be far more important in convoy work than the homogeneity of the types of vessel forming a group. Thus a group might consist of two or three destroyers, which formed the main striking force, four or five of the war-built corvettes, one or two sloops and a number of fishing trawlers which had been converted for anti-submarine work. In early 1941 the total strength of an escort group might, on paper, have been as many as fifteen ships; but the constant need for refits and for dockings to repair the damage caused by the violence of the Atlantic storms, generally kept the actual operational strength down to little more than half that figure.

Though the formation of the permanent escort groups marked a big step in the right direction, formidable difficulties still had to be surmounted before they could be regarded as anything like efficient anti-submarine forces. In the first place, for all the lessons we had learnt in the 1914–18 war, none of the ships which comprised them was well designed for the work they had to carry out. The destroyers, though possessed of a good turn of speed and comparatively powerful armaments, were all old ships, for the more modern ones were all needed to work with our main fleets at home and in the Mediterranean; and those which we had recently taken over from the Americans had undergone even less modernisation than our own. But the most serious weakness of the escort destroyers lay in the fact that none of them had sufficient endurance to cross the Atlantic without refuelling, and we had not yet developed the technique of replenishing them from a tanker in the convoy they were escorting. Thus they always had to leave their convoys with sufficient fuel in hand to reach a shore base. The corvettes had better endurance, but were lightly armed and so lively in a seaway that they taxed their crews very severely indeed. Moreover they were so slow (about 15 knots maximum) that they could not catch a surfaced U-boat. The sloops were comparatively long-endurance ships, and for that reason were more generally employed on the route between Britain and Sierra Leone than in the North Atlantic; while the coal-burning trawlers, though they could keep the sea longer than any other class, were slower and still livelier than the corvettes.

Second only to the deficiencies from which the ships themselves suffered was the problem of finding trained and experienced officers to command them. Astonishing though it may seem in the light of our 1914-18 war experiences, anti-submarine technique and the problems of convoy protection were regarded between the wars as very secondary matters, and little study was devoted to them. Nearly all our fleet exercises were framed to represent engagements between squadrons of heavy ships, and if trade protection entered into them at all it was approached from the point of view of countering surface raiders rather than submarines. Furthermore the anti-submarine branch of the Service was regarded as very much the poor relation of the older branches—gunnery, torpedo or navigation. It thus came to pass that in 1939 we had practically no fund of common experience and doctrine in convoy work to fall back on. Everything had to be studied from the beginning, and experience had to be gained the hard way—from our own mistakes. The Admiralty appointed Commanders, most of whom had experience of small ship work, as Senior Officers of the escort groups, and Lieutenant-Commanders of similar background to the sloops and destroyers;

but it fell mostly to R.N.R. and R.N.V.R. Officers to command the corvettes and trawlers, and they of course had even less experience of convoy work than their R.N. colleagues. A further difficulty arose through the constant shortage of escort vessels making it extremely difficult for senior officers to arrange a programme of steady training for their groups. As soon as one convoy had been brought home they had to prepare to take another one out. Only very rarely could a group exercise as a whole in between convoys, or while on passage by itself. The lack of any common doctrine led, moreover, to senior officers devising their own screening formations, and issuing their own orders on how to deal with any emergency. This may not have mattered if an escort was drawn entirely from one group. But it was, as will be seen later in our story, a common event for ships of two or more groups to have to work together during some stages of a convoy's progress; and when that took place it was all too easy for misunderstandings to arise in, for example, the confused conditions of a night attack by several U-boats. Admiral Noble and his staff well understood the need to standardise practice throughout the ships of his command, and he ultimately issued the Western Approaches Convoy Instructions with that purpose; but at the date with which we are concerned that still lay in the future, and there were still wide variations in the tactical practices of all escort groups.

The group commanders knew full well the need to foster and encourage a strong *esprit de corps* in their ships; and it is a remarkable fact that, even to-day, the group spirit survives among the junior officers and men who served in them. Each group developed its own personality, and there was a healthy rivalry between groups; but in spite of the inadequacies of ships and armaments, and the knowledge that officers and men still had much to learn about their work, all felt completely confident that, if only they could gain contact with their elusive adversaries, they would come out on top. There is indeed no doubt at all that the carefully fostered group spirit had a great deal to do with the success achieved in encounters such as that which led to the capture of U.110.

One recent development which, although still in its infancy in 1941, had greatly increased the confidence of the groups was the advent of an elementary surface radar set. Only a few ships, and those mostly the destroyers, had so far been fitted; but the crews regarded the equipment as little short of magical, and knew that it put them on far more level terms with the surfaced submarine, attacking in darkness, than had been the case when they had to rely solely on visual sighting by look-outs. The radar aerial of those days resembled a bedstead, and was about that size; and as it had to be fitted on the mast it reduced the stability of the ships, and made them roll still more heavily. It even caused the dismasting of several ships which encountered exceptionally violent weather; yet all knew that the scientists and technicians had placed in their hands perhaps the most important anti-submarine development of the whole war. Little could it have been foreseen in those days that, before the war was over, a Group Commander would be able to conduct a search and attack entirely by radar and voice radio from his " plot," without ever emerging on to his bridge.

In the spring of 1941 the homeward North Atlantic traffic was organised into fast (9-knot) convoys from Halifax (HX), and slow (7-knot) convoys from Sydney, Cape Breton Island (SC). In a normal month four of the former and two of the latter would sail for British ports, and four outward convoys (OB) would leave for North America, dispersing in about 35° West to proceed to their several destinations. The main assembly and arrival ports in Britain were Liverpool and the Clyde; for after the fall of France we could make less use of London and the other east coast ports. Such ships as had to proceed to and from the east coast were organised into subsidiary convoys, which were taken round the north of Scotland. Not until July, 1941, were we able to organise end-to-end escort for all outward as well as homeward Atlantic shipping.

To give an idea of the size of the traffic which the Western Approaches Command had to protect, in the first three months of 1941, 687 ships sailed in HX convoys, 306 in SC convoys, and 1,282 in the OB outward series; and in addition to the North Atlantic traffic the same command also had to look after the convoys running to and from Gibraltar and Sierra Leone while they were within its area of responsibility. The north Atlantic escort groups worked mainly from Liverpool and the Clyde, but Londonderry was developing into a very important advanced base, and several groups were based on Hvalfiord in Iceland to relieve the original escorts when they reached the limit of their fuel endurance in about 24° West.

Though the U-boats were reaching ever farther out into the Atlantic from their new bases in western France, in early 1941 none had yet been contacted beyond about 30° West. In consequence it was our practice for an outward convoy only to be escorted to about 35° West, and for the homeward convoys to be given only an anti-raider escort from the east coast of America to that point. In some cases battleships or cruisers fulfilled the latter duty, for the pocket battleship *Scheer*'s attack on convoy HX.84 on 5th November, 1940, and the foray of the battle cruisers *Scharnhorst* and *Gneisenau* in the Atlantic in early 1941 had shown us that only heavy warships could protect the convoys against such enemies. But in many cases only a converted liner, officially and somewhat optimistically described as an Armed Merchant Cruiser, could be provided. These ships called themselves the " suicide squad," and in fact many of them fell victims to the enemy, and especially to the U-boats, against which they were virtually defenceless. In early 1941 they generally broke off from their convoys when the anti-submarine escort was met in mid-Atlantic, steamed to Iceland to refuel and then proceeded west again to pick up another convoy at Halifax. We shall encounter one ship of that type, the former P. & O. liner *Ranpura* later in our story.

CHAPTER IV

The Convoy

ONE OF the unchanging features of maritime war is that convoys always draw enemy commerce raiders to themselves like bees to honey. The reason is the simple one that, once the greatest part of a nation's shipping is sailed in convoy, it is only by finding and attacking one of them that the raiders can fulfil the purpose for which they were fitted out and sent to sea. Nor has the entry of either the submarine or the aircraft into sea warfare altered this feature in the slightest; for both wars of this century have demonstrated very clearly not only how the convoy system enables us to know where to look for the commerce raiders, but how it also produces the opportunity for the escorts to strike back hard at them. Indeed it is true to say that most of the successful actions fought against U-boats took place around convoys, whose slow progress across the ocean often took the form of a continuous battle lasting several days and nights. It is thus inevitable that the story of the capture of U.110 should be closely interwoven with the fate of the convoy which she tried to attack; and to understand how the British success was achieved it is necessary to follow the adventures of the convoy in some detail.

OB.318 was a very typical example of the outward convoys mentioned in the last chapter. The largest section, which finally consisted of seventeen ships, assembled at Liverpool late in April, 1941; and they were to be joined by subsidiary sections assembling at Loch Ewe in north-west Scotland (12 ships), the Clyde (5 ships), and Milford Haven (4 ships).

The ships in Loch Ewe had come from ports on the east coast of Britain, and had already been convoyed round the north of Scotland. All the subsidiary sections were to be sailed to rendezvous with the main convoy at pre-arranged times and positions, and during the passage across the Atlantic three ships were to be detached to Iceland, whence four others would come south to join the convoy. The successful inter-locking of all these movements, and the organisation of the necessary sea and air escorts, plainly demanded very skilful staff work at all the bases concerned. Yet—for the North Atlantic convoys alone—the whole process was carried out at least a dozen times in every month throughout the war.

Throughout the war the Ministry of Transport kept the Admiralty informed regarding the dates when individual merchantmen would be ready to sail, what were their cargoes and whither they were bound; and as all convoys sailed on regular " cycles "—the number of days between the departure of similar convoys—the Admiralty was thus able to start planning each movement well in advance. The preliminary orders for OB.318 were actually issued on the evening of 25th April, 1941, when the Naval authorities in all ports concerned were told the names of the ships detailed for the convoy, their cargoes and their destinations; and in the same message the Admiralty also laid down the route which the convoy was to follow. It was to proceed up the Minches, the sheltered stretch of water between the Hebrides and the west coast of Scotland, and then turn north-west into the Atlantic, passing through a succession of named positions until it reached 50° 50' North 35° West (about midway between Iceland and the southern point of Greenland[1]), where the convoy would break formation, and ships would proceed independently to their several destinations. This first message from the Admiralty set in motion the far-flung and intricate machinery for the organisation of yet another convoy. Next day the

[1] See Map 1 (front end paper).

Naval Control Service Officer in the Mersey, who was the authority responsible to the Admiralty for convoy organisation in that port, signalled that the main section of OB.318 would sail at 3 p.m. (local time) on the 2nd May[1]; and his message was quickly followed by others from the N.C.S.O.s at Milford Haven, the Clyde, and Aultbea (Loch Ewe) stating their intentions with regard to sailing the subsidiary convoys for which they were each responsible. Meanwhile the operational authorities in the naval bases were detailing the escorts for the main convoy and its sub-sections. The destroyer *Vanity*, two anti-submarine trawlers, and an anti-submarine yacht were to bring the Milford Haven section to the rendezvous with the main convoy; the destroyer *Campbeltown* (formerly the U.S. Navy's *Buchanan*), which was to achieve undying fame later in the raid on St. Nazaire on 27th–28th March, 1942) and the A/S trawler *Angle* were to leave with the Clyde section[2], while the destroyer *Newmarket* (the former American *Robinson*) would look after the twelve ships from Loch Ewe for the short distance they had to travel to meet the main convoy in the North Minch shortly before it emerged into the Atlantic. The Flag Officer, Liverpool, had meanwhile nominated the 7th Escort Group to take charge of the convoy for the first part of the ocean passage, and the sloop *Rochester*, with the

[1] On the dates with which we are principally concerned in this narrative (May 1941) local time in the British Isles was Double Summer Time (G.M.T. plus 2 hours). The German Navy was keeping German Summer Time, which was also 2 hours ahead of G.M.T. Because local times varied as our convoy operation moved west it has been thought best to standardise all the times given in the narrative on the basis of G.M.T. Though this gives by far the most convenient standard it does have the disadvantage that it ignores changes in time due to changes in longitude.

[2] The *Angle* actually belonged to the 3rd Escort Group, and was originally intended to rejoin her group in Iceland. During the convoy's passage she was, however, ordered to remain with it and she actually met her consorts at sea on 7th May.

corvettes *Primrose*, *Marigold* and *Nasturtium* of that group, were to leave with the Liverpool section. The Senior Officer of the group, Commander I. H. Bockett-Pugh, in the destroyer *Westcott*, one of the " Admiralty W " class designed for the 1914–18 war and completed in 1918, and the corvettes *Dianthus* and *Auricula* would leave Liverpool about 24 hours after the merchantmen and overtake them off Cape Wrath. By the time the convoy headed out into the Atlantic it would thus be escorted by Bockett-Pugh's full strength, comprising three destroyers, one sloop, five corvettes and a trawler. The destroyers were to top up their fuel tanks in Loch Ewe, and so have the maximum endurance for the westward passage. OB.318's escort was unusually strong in numbers for that period of the war, but only the *Westcott* was fitted with radar, and hers was of a somewhat rudimentary type. Furthermore the two ex-American destroyers, which were the only ships with direction-finding wireless, had not had time to calibrate their sets, and the group thus lacked one of the most valuable means of locating enemy submarines, by taking bearings of their wireless transmissions. But if its technical equipment was far from perfect, in Commander Bockett-Pugh the 7th Escort Group had recently acquired an outstanding leader. He had entered the Navy from Christ's Hospital in 1918, and had served most of the inter-war years in small ships or in naval training establishments. He had been lucky enough to gain early experience of command in a West River gunboat in China, and in 1940 took command of the sloop *Wellington*, which did excellent work on the Gibraltar convoy route. From her he transferred to the *Westcott* early in 1941, and between that date and the end of the war he was awarded three D.S.O.s and once mentioned in despatches.[1] It is hardly surprising that, with such a leader, the 7th Escort Group

[1] The first D.S.O. was awarded to Bockett-Pugh when he, still in the *Westcott*, sank U.581 off the Azores on 2nd February, 1942; the second was for sinking a French submarine off Oran during the

should quickly gain a reputation for efficient convoy work, and for striking hard blows at any enemy which came within its reach.

But the organisation of the initial escorts for OB.318 was not the end of the preparations which the Western Approaches Command had to make. No. 15 Group of Coastal Command had been given the course which the convoy would take, and the orders for its departure, when they were issued by the Admiralty; and a representative of the Group was always on duty in the operations room at Western Approaches Command Headquarters. Thus the Royal Air Force was able to make its own plans to meet the Admiralty's needs by providing the convoy with air escort until it passed outside the range of the home-based aircraft. At the time with which we are dealing this was only about 600 miles; but other aircraft flying from Iceland bases, which formed part of No. 15 Group, would take over the responsibility when the convoy came within their range. A second important measure was that Admiral Noble detailed the 3rd Escort Group under Commander A. J. Baker-Cresswell, which had recently arrived in Reykjavik from another convoy operation, to relieve Bockett-Pugh's group at a rendezvous some 150 miles south of Reykjavik in Iceland on the evening of the 7th May. We will return to the composition of the 3rd Escort Group, and its actions while escorting OB.318 later; for we must now look at the merchantmen forming the convoy a little more closely. Of the 42 ships originally nominated for OB.318 five were not ready in time; but the Dutch ocean tug *Zwarte Zee* was added, making 38 ships in all. Their total tonnage was 204,811 Gross Register Tons, and no less than six different nations were represented in the convoy. The Dutch and Norwegians each owned three of the ships, one was Swedish (the only neutral ship present) another was of Belgian registry, and Greece was

North African landings on 8th November, 1942, and the third was for his services in the Normandy landings of June 1944.

also represented by one ship. All the remaining twenty-nine belonged to British shipowners, or were sailing under charter to one of them or to the Ministry of Transport. In size the ships in the convoy varied from the tiny short-sea trader *Atlantic Coast* of 890 tons to the China Mutual Steam Navigation Company's fine passenger-cargo steamer *Ixion* of 10,263 tons. No less than five of the convoy were tankers, bound for the West Indian oil ports.[1]

The speeds of which different ships were theoretically capable varied from 9 to $12\frac{1}{2}$ knots; but the speed of the convoy would, of course, have to be the speed of the slowest ship, and it was unlikely that more than 8 knots could be maintained while steaming in formation. No less than sixteen of the convoy were in ballast for the outward journey, having discharged their cargoes of food, war stores or raw materials in Britain and been unable to find a return cargo. The loaded ships had a wide variety of cargoes, such as clay, coal, chalk and wood pulp for American or Canadian ports, military stores for West Africa or the Middle East, and general cargoes for the United States. The latter included specially valuable exports, such as whisky, which we continued to send to the United States in order to earn precious dollars. The final destinations of the merchantmen, for which they would steer as soon as the convoy dispersed, covered almost the whole world. Though several were bound only for the east coasts of America and Canada, others were to round the Cape of Good Hope, or pass through the Panama Canal into the Pacific, there to discharge what they carried and to load again with Britain's most urgent needs. Buenos Aires, Freetown, Durban, Curaçao, Jamaica, Lagos, and many other ports were shown as the final destination of one or more ships. The convoy was indeed a remarkable epitome of the world-wide seaborne traffic on which our peacetime prosperity depends, and which, in time of war,

[1] See Diagram 3 (back end paper) for the composition and formation of Convoy OB.318 on sailing.

keeps our factories in production and our fighting services supplied with all their multifarious needs. As evidence of the dangers of the service on which they were now engaged, the individual distinguishing marks of the various lines were no longer worn, and most ships were painted a nondescript grey. Even their names had been obliterated, and all except the neutral Swedish ship were defensively armed. Twenty-eight of them carried an old naval 4-inch gun mounted at the stern for defence against a pursuing submarine, while nine had 12-pounder dual-purpose (anti-aircraft or low-angle) weapons. Recent enemy air attacks on our merchantmen had caused the Admiralty to provide some form of anti-aircraft gun or device to as many ships as possible, desperately short though we were of all such weapons. Ten of the convoy had received 40 mm. Bofors guns, which actually belonged to the Army and were manned by military crews drawn from a recently organised formation known as the Maritime Anti-Aircraft Regiment. These guns, together with their crews, were generally removed at the first convenient port of call, and then transferred to a homeward-bound ship. But, in addition to the Bofors, all ships carried from two to six light machine-guns, and eighteen of them were fitted to fly kites on wire cables—a device which we had found useful for scaring off low-flying aircraft. Each ship carried a number of trained men, most of whom were Naval or Royal Marine pensioners or reservists, drawn from the Admiralty's world-wide Defensively Equipped Merchant Ship (D.E.M.S.) organisation; and they provided the key numbers at the guns. But the Merchant Navy officers and men had themselves been receiving an increasing amount of training in gunnery, and in most ships they were capable of using at least the lighter weapons at a moment's notice. We had indeed found that, in the conditions which had prevailed since the crisis of June, 1940, a merchant ship had to be prepared to defend herself at all hours of the day or night; and that could only be accomplished by virtually all her deck officers and men being trained to handle and use the weapons provided by the Admiralty.

The organisation of the convoy, and the plans made for its defence, were discussed at convoy conferences held at Liverpool and in the subsidiary ports before each section sailed. The masters of all the merchantmen were invariably present, as was the Commodore of the convoy, the Senior Officer of the escort, the Naval Control Service Officer in the port, and a representative of No. 15 Group. The Masters of ships had previously received written orders regarding the formation and sailing of the convoy, together with the necessary signal instructions, and at the conference the chairman outlined the plans, and the Commodore gave his intentions should an emergency, such as a submarine contact, arise. Questions were then invited from the ships' Masters. Sometimes Admiral Noble himself took the chair at the main conference in Liverpool; but more commonly it would be his Chief of Staff, or the Naval Control Service Officer, who fulfilled that function. The atmosphere was entirely informal, and the intimate way in which plans and problems were discussed across the table undoubtedly reinforced the confidence of the Masters that everything possible would be done for the protection of their ships, and that their own problems were sympathetically understood by the Royal Navy.

In the narrow waters of the Minches the convoy could not steam in its ocean formation, and would therefore proceed in two loosely organised columns. But as soon as it emerged into the Atlantic ships would take up their final stations. Our convoy was actually organised in nine columns, each consisting of four or five ships; and their positions in the convoy were identified by two figure symbols. The first figure was the number of the column, counting from the left of the formation, and the second signified the position of a ship in the column, counting from its head. Thus Number 84 would be the fourth ship in Column 8. This system had been made standard for all convoy operations, and enabled ships to be quickly identified and spoken to. Their peacetime names, though shown on the Convoy Form, now gave place to the more impersonal numbers. The formation and numbering of OB.318 are shown on the diagram at the end of this book. Ships in column were to keep station at two cables (400 yards) distance, while the spaces between columns were normally to be five cables (1,000 yards) if U-boat attacks threatened, but might be shortened to three cables (600 yards) if enemy bombers were the greater danger; for we had found that the closer formation enabled ships to render each other mutual support in the event of air attack. In April, 1941, the practice of zig-zagging in formation, according to a pre-arranged plan, was abolished for slow convoys. Instead the Commodore would employ " evasive steering " to keep his charges clear of waters where U-boats were known or suspected to be lying in wait, or to shake off a shadowing enemy. In addition, if a sudden emergency arose—such as a ship being torpedoed—the whole convoy could be turned together 40 degrees at a time in either direction by flag or light signal from the Commodore's ship, or by siren signal in low visibility.

The reader will realise that accurate station keeping and safe manœuvring in formation placed a heavy strain on the Masters and watch officers of the merchantmen, especially in heavy weather. With ships of widely varying size and performance it needed constant vigilance to maintain correct station, and it is not surprising that hair-raising escapes from collision were quite frequent, and serious accidents by no means uncommon. Yet all our experience proved that ships in convoy were, except in the case of those possessed of an outstanding turn of speed, far safer from either submarine or air attack than ships sailing independently; and most Masters, though they disliked convoy with varying degrees of intensity, came to recognise this. The Admiralty and Senior Officers of escort groups did all they could to discourage the practice of straggling astern of a convoy, which was notoriously dangerous; and although the habit was never entirely eradicated it became rarer as the war progressed, and the steady toll taken of ships which broke formation became more widely known. Many convoys made their passages without a ship breaking the formation, and manœuvred with a precision which called forth the admiration of the escorts. Others did less well, and it was these that were most liable to run into serious trouble.

The Commodore of OB.318 was Rear-Admiral (Retd.) W. B. Mackenzie, and he and his small signal staff sailed in the 5,108-ton British ship *Colonial*, owned by the Charente Steamship Company, which was carrying a general cargo to Sierra Leone and Capetown. Her position in the convoy was at the head of Column No. 4. The Vice-Commodore was Captain E. Rees, Master of the *British Prince* bound for Halifax, and the Rear-Commodore was the Master of the *Burma* whose destination was Capetown. These two ships were stationed at the heads of Columns No. 2 and 6 respectively, and their Masters would take over responsibility for the convoy if casualties eliminated the more senior officers. Rear-Admiral Mackenzie was one of the gallant band of retired Flag Officers who returned to serve in the Royal Naval Reserve as Commodores of ocean convoys. No less than 21 of them were lost at sea during the war—probably a higher percentage of casualties than was suffered by any other branch of the Service. Mackenzie was born in Dumbartonshire in 1885, joined the *Britannia* at the age of 14, and specialised in Torpedo as a Lieutenant. At the Battle of Jutland he was serving in the ill-fated battleship *Royal Oak*, and after the first war he was executive officer of the *Emperor of India* during a commission which the survivors of her company still look back on happily. As a Captain he commanded several light cruisers and the aircraft carrier *Hermes* between the wars, and played a big part in organising anti-submarine training and starting a specialist branch in that vital subject while commanding the shore establishment formed for that purpose at Portland. His last appointment was as Director of Torpedoes and Mining in the Admiralty at the time when, in the 1930's, the reluctance of the government to face the rising truculence of the dictators and provide the funds needed for re-armament was causing the greatest anxieties in Service circles. It was Mackenzie's lot to try to prepare his branch for the clash which appeared increasingly probable, while denied the means to do so effectively. His strength of character and unshakable calm in face of difficulties or danger made him an ideal man to work with and help the Merchant Navy when, soon after the outbreak of the second war, he was asked to serve as Commodore of convoys.

Convoy OB.318's journey started uneventfully on the afternoon of 2nd May. The subsidiary sections all joined up at their appointed times and places, and the passage up the Minches was made in fine weather. As soon as the Liverpool, Milford, Clyde and Loch Ewe sections had cleared harbour the Naval Control Service officers at the ports reported their departure, and also the final destinations and expected dates of arrival of the individual ships. In the Operations Intelligence Centre at the Admiralty and on the plot at Derby House, Liverpool, where Admiral Noble had his headquarters, special symbols indicating the convoy's position were now in place on the vast wall maps, and strings had been stretched across the ocean to show its intended course. Against the convoy symbols were shown the names of the escorts, and from now onwards a constant watch was kept on the progress of the operation.

During its northward passage through the coastal waters the convoy was given strong and continuous air escort as long as daylight lasted; for the Germans had recently been making frequent bombing attacks on our inshore shipping, and we also knew that some U-boats were patrolling not very far outside the Hebrides. On 3rd and 4th May four Ansons of No. 48 Squadron, flying from Islay and Stornoway, were continuously with the convoy, and on the latter day they were reinforced by a fighter escort of four Blenheims from No. 248 Squadron, whose base was at Wick in north-east Scotland. That evening, as the convoy rounded the Butt of Lewis, the northern cape of the Hebrides, a night-flying Whitley from Wick patrolled overhead. On arrival it was greeted by a short burst of fire from one of the escort vessels—which fortunately did no damage. It was always difficult to identify friendly aircraft at dusk, but the Navy insisted that it must be free to open fire on any aircraft which closed within 1,500 yards. It may be that the Whitley inadvertently came too close, but the fury of the airmen who were all too frequently shot at by those whom they were endeavouring to protect can easily be understood.

At 10.15 p.m., on the 4th, when the convoy was at the northern entrance to the Minches, Commander Bockett-Pugh joined up in the *Westcott*, and took command. The weather was calm and warm, the ships of the convoy had taken up their appointed stations under Commodore Mackenzie's watchful eye, the escort assumed its screening disposition and course was set N. 74° W. (true). The *Westcott* being the only escort fitted with radar, Bockett-Pugh spent the night circling his charges. He thus preserved freedom to take station at any time two miles from the convoy in the most probable direction of attack. His orders to his group were that at dusk each evening (about 11 p.m. local time) he himself would sweep ahead, while the *Newmarket* and *Campbeltown* did likewise astern and on the quarters, and the *Primrose* and *Nasturtium* searched to ten miles on each beam of the convoy. Any shadowing U-boats would thus be forced to submerge, which would add to their difficulty in carrying out a night attack. The searching ships were to be back with the convoy by midnight, and at dawn (about 5 a.m. local time) the whole escort would change

The Italian submarine
Galileo Galilei
being towed into Aden,
after her capture
by H.M.S. *Moonstone*
and other ships,
19th June, 1940

e surrender of U.570 to Hudson S. of No. 269 Squadron
Coastal Command, 27th August, 1941

The capture of the
Italian submarine *Perla*
by H.M.S. *Hyacinth*,
off Beirut,
9th July, 1942.
The British prize crew
is working the submarine
from her conning tower
while the Italian
survivors sit on the
fore deck.

The Italian submarine *Bronzo* in tow by H.M.S. *Seaham*,
off Augusta, Sicily, 12th July, 1943

H.M.C.S. *Chilliwack* boarding U. 744 in the Atlantic,
in March, 1944
The corvette's masts can just be seen beyond the
U-boat.

Convoy OB.318
on passage south of Iceland, May, 1941

H.M.S. *Bulldog*, senior officer's ship, 3rd Escort Group, leaving Iceland to meet convoy OB.318, 7th May, 1941

Commander
A. J. Baker-Cresswell, R.N.,
Senior Officer 3rd Escort Group
on the bridge of H.M.S. *Bulldog*

H.M.S. *Bulldog*. Taken before the war

H.M.S. *Aubrietia*

U.110 breaks surface. H.M.S. *Bulldog* lowering her whaler with boarding party. Taken from H.M.S. *Aubrietia*

Survivors from U.110 in the water.
Taken from H.M.S. *Aubrietia*

H.M.S. *Bulldog* taking U.110 in tow

Sub-Lieutenant D. E. Balme, R.N.,
leader of H.M.S. *Bulldog's*
boarding party

Kapitänleutnant
Fritz-Julius Lemp of U.110.
The Iron Cross he is wearing
was found on board U.110
and was returned
to his sister
by Captain Baker-Cresswell
in 1958

from its night anti-submarine disposition to day anti-aircraft stations.[1]

It is difficult to be precise regarding the exact screening diagram ordered by Bockett-Pugh; for, as with virtually all escort groups at that time, it was peculiar to his own command and no copy of his orders has survived. It is likely, however, that while he himself in the *Westcott* preserved complete freedom of manœuvre around the convoy, his other two destroyers (the *Campbeltown* and *Newmarket*) were stationed a mile ahead of it, the sloop *Rochester* was the same distance astern, and the five corvettes and the trawler *Angle* were on the bows and beam of the convoy, three on each side. We know, at any rate, that the 7th Escort Group was in such a formation when it turned the convoy over to the 3rd Escort Group on the evening of the 7th May.[2]

Throughout the daylight hours of the 5th, Coastal Command aircraft continued their vigil above and around the convoy as it steamed steadily west in good formation. In fact the records of No. 15 Group show that the convoy was far better looked after than either the merchantmen or the surface escort realised at the time; for a Whitley of No. 612 Squadron, five Hudsons of Nos. 220 and 269 Squadrons and a continuous escort of Blenheim fighters from Wick all accompanied it throughout the day. It is, indeed, a common experience for surface vessels not to realise how closely they are guarded by friendly aircraft, much of whose activity may take place at the limit of visibility, or even beyond the horizon. A good example of this phenomenon occurred that afternoon when, at 2.35 p.m. Hudson O of No. 269 Squadron, commanded by Sergeant C. H. Eatley, sighted a U-boat on the surface some fifty miles astern of the convoy while flying outwards to join the air escort. This was almost certainly U.141, which was proceeding back to

[1] On 5th May off the Butt of Lewis sunrise was at 6.23 a.m., and sunset at 10.20 p.m. British Double Summer Time.

[2] See p. 86 and Map No. 1 (front end paper).

Norway round the north of Scotland after a patrol in the Atlantic. Sergeant Eatley at once dropped three depth charges and reported the sighting, whereupon the Commander-in-Chief, Home Fleet, ordered two of his destroyers, the *Electra* and *Escapade*, which were on the way to meet convoy HX.122, to make for the position at high speed to co-operate with the aircraft, and No. 15 Group sent out a Whitley to join the searchers. But the U-boat had not been sighted again by the time that the destroyers had to break off the hunt to meet their convoy.

The Admiralty's assessment of Sergeant Eatley's attack was that the U-boat was " probably seriously damaged," which we now know to have been very near the mark; for U.141's report states that " two bombs (*sic*) fell 20 metres to starboard," and caused such damage to a fuel tank and to the diesel engine cooling system that her Captain reported to U-boat head-quarters that he could not reach Bergen. Dönitz therefore ordered him to make for Lorient, where he arrived safely on 11th May. The *Westcott* had also picked up Sergeant Eatley's sighting report, but the enemy was already well astern of the convoy and Commander Bockett-Pugh did not therefore consider it necessary to take evasive action. It is plain, however, that some earlier sign of U-boat activity in the way of the convoy had reached Derby House; for at 9.38 a.m. that morning Admiral Noble diverted it to the south of the track originally ordered by the Admiralty " to avoid possible U-boat threat."[1] It is possible that this prescient action kept OB.318 clear of trouble from U.147, which was not very far away at the time.

That same afternoon the Western Approaches Command arranged for the change-over of escorts in mid-Atlantic, by ordering the Naval Officer in Charge, Iceland, to sail the 3rd Escort Group so as to meet the convoy in 61° 07' North 23° 37' West (about 200 miles south of Reykjavik) at 6 p.m.

[1] See Map No. 1 (front end paper).

on the 7th. Admiral Noble signalled what the convoy's course should be at that time, and gave the direction from which the new escort was to approach the rendezvous, thus minimising the risk of the convoy and the relief escort missing each other.

With the ten ships of the 7th Escort Group now disposed around our convoy, their Asdic sets constantly probing the depths, while the watchkeepers in Derby House moved the symbol indicating the convoy's progress every four hours, and the Admiralty's centralised intelligence organisation listened alertly for the slightest sign of the enemy they knew to be lurking on the convoy's route, it is time that we looked on " the other side of hill " to see what was happening in Dönitz's headquarters at Lorient, and how the U-boats then in the North Atlantic were disposed.

CHAPTER V

The Enemies in the Way

ON 5TH May, 1941, when OB.318 emerged from the Minches into the North Atlantic, there were probably nine U-boats on patrol in the Atlantic north of latitude 55 degrees.[1] Three of these were cruising in about 25° West, but all the others were in the north-western approaches to the British Isles, which we may define as covering a 90-degree arc of 600 miles radius with its centre in the Clyde. There were five more in the south-western approaches, and several others were still further south, approaching or leaving the Bay of Biscay bases. Two of the northern boats (U.75 and U.123) were actually withdrawing towards the French coast, but two others (U.556 and U.111) had recently left Germany for the Atlantic by the northern route round the Shetlands and Faeroes, and reached their patrol areas within the next two or three days. The total strength available to work against our convoy between 5th and 9th May thus remained fairly constant; but as only four boats (U.94, U.110, U.201 and U.556) were actually involved in attacks on it we need not concern ourselves greatly with the movements of the other five.

On the day that our convoy took up its ocean formation off Cape Wrath Dönitz's staff reviewed future prospects in the Atlantic Battle. They noted in their War Diary that our convoys " generally dispersed in longitudes up to 25° West," and they therefore deduced that " whereas the greatest

[1] The movements of U.20 at this time are doubtful, and the total may therefore have been ten.

concentration (of British shipping) would be found off the New-
foundland Banks or in the approaches to the North Channel
to the Irish Sea, the greatest *spread* occurred between 25° and
30° West." As our homeward convoys were generally being
met by an anti-submarine escort in about 30° West, and our
outward convoys were dispersing in the same longitude, the
U-boat Command's deductions were, broadly speaking,
correct. What the enemy particularly wanted to do was to
catch our homeward shipping before it was joined by a close
escort, and our outward convoys after their escorts had withdrawn; for the merchantmen would then be at their most
vulnerable. U-boat Headquarters were perturbed about the
increasing strength and effectiveness of our escorts. " Defence
by (British) sea and air forces has been observed to an increasing
degree," they noted on 6th May. " These defensive measures,"
they continued, " have resulted in boats being driven off in
various cases, even though they managed to approach a convoy
. . . There have been no great successes lately." On the same
day Dönitz's staff repeated their frequent complaints about
the failure of the Luftwaffe to co-operate effectively. Such
air reports as were received were, so they said, generally
valueless, because of the inaccuracy of the positions given.
Thus " the Luftwaffe gives no help in guiding the U-boats
to the enemy."

For operational purposes the U-boat Command divided
the Atlantic into a number of zones, each designated by a two-
letter symbol; and the zones were all sub-divided into a number of rectangles, each of which was identified by two figures.
The rectangles could be further sub-divided into smaller
spaces, to enable a spot in the ocean to be exactly pin-pointed,
but these were not marked on the special charts issued to all
U-boats. The principle on which the German charts were
constructed is shown in the diagram below.

By a simple signal such as " Convoy in AK.2799 " Dönitz's
headquarters could indicate to the patrolling U-boats the

SECTION OF GERMAN GRIDDED U-BOAT CHART FOR THE ATLANTIC

Diagram 1

13	14	23	24	33	34
15	16	25	26	35	36
17	18	27	28	37	38
19	01	29	02	39	03

Diagram 2

1	2	3
4	5	6
7	8	9

AK2799

Diagram 2 is an enlargement of square 27 in Diagram 1

presence and position of any convoy or naval force; and we could only identify the threatened units by measuring the direction from which the U-boats had signalled to their base. But capture of one of the German gridded charts would, of course, at once give us a more accurate idea of what their intentions were. Surface ships and aircraft could then be sent to search for the enemies with good prospects of success, and threatened convoys could be diverted on to safer courses. It will not need much imagination to appreciate the scope of the benefits thereby gained to our cause.

It is with Zones AM, AL and AK on the German charts that we are here principally concerned; for they covered the Atlantic Ocean between latitudes 51° and 61° North and longitudes 5° to 40° West. Virtually all our North Atlantic shipping thus had to pass through those zones.

On 6th May Dönitz ordered six boats (U.93, 94, 97, 98, 201 and 556) to proceed to square AK in the central Atlantic where they were to be joined later by U.109 and 111 from Germany and U.43 and 74 from France; but in fact this dangerous concentration in one area was not fully implemented, because some of the boats were diverted to other duties. In spite of his lack of confidence in the Luftwaffe's co-operation Dönitz asked at the same time for reconnaissance flights by the long-range FW.200 aircraft stationed at Stavanger in Norway and near Bordeaux, with the object of reporting traffic approaching or leaving the British Isles. Since the fall of France the Italian Navy had been anxious that its submarines should play a part in the Atlantic battle, and a number of them had come to French bases for the purpose. But the Germans had found from experience that, if they tried to co-ordinate operations with the Italian submarines, the latter were liable to be more of a handicap than an advantage; and on the same day Dönitz allocated to them an area well to the south of our main convoy routes. " Here," he remarked scathingly, " they cannot adversely affect our own operations."

Early on 6th two German reconnaissance aircraft reported an inward-bound convoy in about 60° North 13° West; but their fixes were about 100 miles apart, and did not therefore greatly help the U-boat command. They must in fact have been reporting either the fast convoy HX.122 or the slow convoy SC.29, or possibly both of them; for they were both approaching the west of Scotland at that time.[1] At 1.57 p.m. next day, the 7th, U.95 reported a convoy, almost certainly SC.29, to have been 120 miles west of the Hebrides at 8.40 that morning, on a south-easterly course. Dönitz realised that the convoy had by that time progressed too far to the east to enable an attack to be organised, and he therefore took no action; but in the Admiralty U.95's signal had very interesting repercussions. We will return to the matter shortly, for we must see how our convoy had meanwhile been progressing since we left it steering north-west from the Butt of Lewis on the evening of the 5th.

That day Commodore Mackenzie seized the opportunity to exercise the merchantmen in carrying out emergency turns in formation. This was by far the most likely manœuvre to be called for, and was never an easy one to accomplish without losing cohesion—especially by night. At 4 p.m. course was altered from N. 80° W. (true, to S. 89° W. in accordance with Admiral Noble's alteration to the route originally given by the Admiralty. The night of the 5th–6th passed quietly, with the escorts carrying out their usual dusk searches; but two evasive alterations of course were made during the dark hours with the object of shaking off any pursuers. At dawn on the 6th the convoy was steering N. 76° W. (true), and there was still a Coastal Command Whitley patrolling watchfully overhead; but she had to return to base soon afterwards, and during the rest of the day Coastal Command could not provide any close air escorts. The reason was that No. 15 Group was very busy protecting the homeward-bound convoys HX.122 and

[1] See Map 1 (front end paper).

SC.29, either or both of which had, as we have already seen, been reported by the enemy; and on this day the air escorts of SC.29 actually had several engagements with German long-range FW.200 reconnaissance-bombers. But OB.318 was not entirely neglected; for Catalinas and Whitleys flew several sweeps from their Scottish bases out to the north-west, and on one of them our convoy was sighted and reported to be in no trouble of any sort. The only interesting event to take place around the convoy on the 6th was the sighting by the *Rochester* of a floating torpedo. Bockett-Pugh lowered a boat from the *Westcott* and picked it up successfully, with the intention of forwarding it to our technical intelligence organisation.

Throughout the following night the convoy plodded steadily on at 8 knots. By the morning of the 7th it had got beyond the range of No. 15 Group's Hudsons working from Scotland, but was escorted for part of the forenoon by one of the Sunderlands stationed in Iceland, until the threat of fog at its base caused it to be recalled. This was unfortunate, since had the Sunderland been able to stay with the convoy she might well have sighted, later in the day, a slim, dark shape lying low in the water ahead of the convoy's track; and she might thus have been able to give warning of the presence of Kapitänleutnant Herbert Kuppisch's U.94.

At 8.30 a.m. on the 7th the Iceland section, consisting of the merchantmen *Iron Baron* and *Atlantic Coast* and the Dutch ocean tug *Zwarte Zee* left the convoy, and proceeded in company towards Reykjavik. Shortly afterwards the *Westcott* sighted an empty lifeboat, bearing the name *Terje Viken*. Throughout the war the Atlantic was all too full of such flotsam; and often it could have told tragic tales. In the present case the boat undoubtedly came from the United Whalers' Company 20,638-ton factory ship, which had been sunk about 400 miles to the east on 7th March. During the day the escort vessels also sighted and sank several mines, which had probably broken adrift from the barrage we had been laying between Iceland

and the Faeroes. Ever since the summer of 1940 we had been expending a considerable effort on this enormous minefield. Its object was to impede the passage of U-boats into the Atlantic by the northern route; but we now know that it was a singularly unprofitable undertaking, for during the entire war only one enemy was sunk in it.

During the forenoon of the 7th Bockett-Pugh's ships several times reported Asdic contacts, and in some cases attacked them. But by the early afternoon the group commander became convinced that they " were all hunting whales, or possibly patches of cold water," and he ordered the hunters to rejoin the convoy. Fifty-two depth charges were, however, expended —a depletion of their outfits which some of the ships were to regret later.

We saw earlier how U.95 made a sighting report on one of our homeward convoys (HX.122 or SC.29) far to the east of OB.318 at 1.57 p.m. on the 7th. The Germans always prefixed such messages with an accented letter E in the morse code (dot dot dash dot dot), and we called them " E-Bar messages " from the British custom of writing the accented E with a bar over it thus (ē). As soon as such a message was heard by the Admiralty's interception service, and the direction-finding stations had taken bearings of the transmission, so enabling us to fix the sender's position approximately, it was plotted in the Submarine Tracking Room. A glance at the plot would now probably indicate which convoy the enemy had sighted, and action would at once be taken to warn the escort and to divert the convoy. But in the present case things did not work out quite that way. The listening stations picked up U.95's report correctly, but the *direction* from which it came was about the same as that of our convoy, and the Admiralty therefore estimated that it was OB.318 which had been reported. Actually it was some 325 miles to the west of U.95's position at the time. Had the Admiralty been able to decode the message such a mistake would have been impossible;

for we now know that U.95 reported the convoy she had sighted to be steering *south-east*. The result was that, at 3.04 p.m. the Admiralty sent an " Immediate " signal to Bockett-Pugh, and also to Baker-Cresswell's 3rd Escort Group, which had left Iceland early that morning to join the convoy, saying that OB.318, or possibly Baker-Cresswell's ships, had been reported by a U-boat. At the same time the Admiralty also used its powers of direct operational control to order the convoy to make an evasive turn to starboard until it reached latitude 62° North, and then to steer due west. The message was received by the *Westcott* and also by Baker-Cresswell's *Bulldog* at 3.51 p.m., and the former communicated it to the Commodore. About an hour later Mackenzie wheeled his convoy round from N. 70° W. (true) to N. 42° W. Bockett-Pugh did not consider the turn drastic enough, and wanted the Commodore to alter further to starboard; but Mackenzie adhered to his decision. Baker-Cresswell also expected the convoy to make a bigger alteration, and allowed for it to be steering about N. 27° W. when he started to search for it.

It is impossible to say whether, had this alteration not been made, the convoy would have been missed by U.94; but it certainly appears that it caused OB.318 to steer directly into Kuppisch's arms, for at 6.05 p.m. he sighted the merchantmen's funnel smoke to the east. As Baker-Cresswell had successfully made his rendezvous only twenty minutes earlier, the 3rd Escort Group was granted little time in which to prepare for trouble.

CHAPTER VI

The 3rd Escort Group and
the First Attack, 7th May

JOE BAKER-CRESSWELL was born in London on 2nd February, 1901, while most of his family were watching Queen Victoria's funeral procession from the windows of their London home. It was thus just before his fortieth birthday that he was appointed, in January, 1941, to command the 3rd Escort Group. Such an appointment had been his heart's desire ever since the beginning of the war; and it was the combination of his own determination and a chance meeting with Admiral Noble at the entrance to the Admiralty which brought it to him. He came of a very old Northumbrian family on whose former estate stands Cresswell Tower, which is known to have belonged to them since 1190. The estates were, however, all bequeathed outside the family by his father when he died in 1921, two years after Joe had joined the Navy from Gresham's School in Norfolk. As a Lieutenant he specialised in navigation, and subsequently served as navigator in a wide variety of classes of ship, from submarine to battleship. He thus gained experience which was to stand him in very good stead during the war. After graduating as a Commander in the Naval Staff College he went on to the R.A.F. Staff College; but his course there came to a premature end in August, 1939, when it became obvious that war with Germany might break out at any moment. The combination of wide sea experience, including handling many different classes of ship, with staff training marked him for early command; and the senior officers under whom he had served had no doubt that his quick brain and ripe intellect, supported by a calmness of decision and readiness to take responsibility fitted him for high posts in the Service. But it was to be some time before he gained the chance to make his mark at sea; for just before the outbreak of war he was hustled out to Cairo in deep secrecy to become the naval member of the Middle East Joint Planning Staff. The work was very interesting, the more so because he had to act as liaison officer between General Wavell and Admiral Cunningham in all the great joint undertakings of the early days; but a shore appointment in time of war did not at all suit Baker-Cresswell's temperament, and he soon became impatient for a command of his own. Neither a hectic trip to Crete and Greece at the time of the Italian attack in October, 1940, nor the unwillingness of Admiral Cunningham to permit changes among the staff, did anything to damp his ardour or assuage his thirst for action at sea. His opportunity came quite suddenly when, in November, 1940, the Chief of Staff telephoned from Alexandria to ask if he would like to take command of the 10,000-ton supply ship *Breconshire* and act as Commodore of an important convoy (called MW.4) bound for Malta, in which she was to sail almost immediately. The bait was attractive, for Baker-Cresswell was told that he could return to Britain in the battleship *Ramillies* after revictualling Malta; and the fact that the *Breconshire*'s cargo included 6,000 tons of oil, 600 tons of petrol and a large quantity of ammunition did not worry him one whit. Escorted and covered by the entire Mediterranean Fleet she arrived safely on 26th November, and discharged her somewhat inflammable cargo. Baker-Cresswell then joined the *Ramillies*, and in her took part in Admiral Somerville's action with the Italian Fleet off Cape Spartivento (Sardinia) on 27th November. But the *Ramillies* was subsequently held at Gibraltar, and his impatience to get home was thus aroused again. He therefore transferred to the old aircraft carrier *Argus*, which safely reached the Clyde by a circuitous route in December. Baker-Cresswell then came to London to seek a new appointment from the Admiralty, and as he was entering the Whitehall building he encountered Admiral Noble, under whom he had served before the war. He explained the purpose of his visit to the Admiral, who at once said, " Leave it to me "; and the Commander therefore penetrated no further into the Admiralty. A short while later he received an appointment to command the 3rd Escort Group. We need not here follow the details of the group's early operations, but the recollections of all who served in it confirm how quickly its new senior officer imposed his personality and determination on his ships, and made them into a highly efficient, integrated striking force. One of his juniors, Lieutenant-Commander V. F. Smith, R.N.R., who commanded the corvette *Aubrietia* in those days, and who played a big part in the defence of convoy OB.318, wrote to the author in 1958 from the tanker *British Skill*, of which he was the Master, to say that " The 3rd Escort Group was a grand group to work with. . . . Should you be writing to Captain Baker-Cresswell I would be most happy if you would send him my sincerest regards and good wishes."

As soon as he had taken over his new command in 1941 Baker-Cresswell seized every chance to improve the training of individual ships, and of his group as a whole. He tried out new convoy screening formations, exercised his ships in co-ordinated counter-attacks on submarines, and arranged frequent practices for the Asdic operators, and for the crews of the guns and depth charge rails and throwers. He also studied camouflage as a means to improve the chances of surprising an enemy at dusk or dawn—always the most critical hours in convoy work—and finally he painted his ships pale mauve, which he found the best aid to invisibility in the Atlantic in spring and summer. When winter came, however, he changed the group colour to white, which proved far superior in such conditions. These colour schemes, first adopted in the 3rd Escort Group, were widely used later on—including in the Mediterranean, where the mauve shade became known as " Mountbatten pink." As an individual mark for his group Baker-Cresswell painted the blue and yellow chequers of the old naval " Flag 3 " around the top of his ships' funnels, and although unkind remarks were heard about " custard tins " and " Scottish policemen " that fashion too was soon copied by other groups.

In April the group was well up to strength, and consisted of three destroyers, six corvettes and three trawlers. The Senior Officer's pendant was worn by the destroyer *Bulldog*, which was a 1,360-ton ship, and one of a class of eight ordered under the 1928 naval programme. She was built on the Tyne by Messrs. Swan Hunter, and first commissioned in 1930. Her armaments originally consisted of eight torpedo-tubes in quadruple mountings, and four 4.7-inch guns; but both guns and torpedo-tubes were reduced during the war to enable more depth charges to be carried. Early in April the 3rd Escort Group was detailed to take a slow convoy out from Liverpool by the northern route; but Baker-Cresswell did not sail on that operation. There were experienced R.N. Lieutenant-Commanders in command of the destroyers *Amazon* and *Ambuscade*, and when his ship was due for boiler cleaning or refit he always felt perfectly confident to leave one of them in charge of a convoy. Moreover Admiral Noble had decided to transfer the group's base from Liverpool to Iceland, and the prospect of a prolonged stay in northern waters obviously made it necessary for the senior officer's ship to be in first-class condition. The interval for boiler cleaning gave Baker-Cresswell three days well-earned leave at his Hampshire home, after which he took the *Bulldog* to Hvalfiord, fuelled and then at once went to sea again to join the rest of his group, who had just been released from escorting the outward convoy that the *Bulldog* had missed. The next job

was to meet a homeward convoy off south-west Iceland;
but the group had to search as far to the west as 31° in very
stormy weather before they found the merchantmen, which
were 18 hours behind schedule. Four days later Baker-
Cresswell turned his charges over to the group from Britain
which was to escort the convoy during the final stretch home;
but by that time the fuel situation in his ships was critical.
He just managed to coax them back to Iceland, where the
destroyers arrived on 5th May with only a few tons of fuel
left and the trawlers with no coal at all in their bunkers! That
experience was typical of the problems which beset the commanders of the mid-ocean groups in those days. Nor was there
any appreciable interval between convoys; for, as we have
already seen, the 3rd Escort Group had meanwhile been ordered
to meet OB.318 on 7th May. Baker-Cresswell was, however,
this time able to give his men a short run ashore at Reykjavik,
and he took the *Bulldog* round there from Hvalfiord on the 6th.
The blazing lights of a town in which the black-out was, as
yet, unknown seemed very strange to the British sailors! In
harbour was the former P. & O. liner *Ranpura* (Acting Captain
H. T. W. Pawsey), now an Armed Merchant Cruiser, and one
of the self-styled " suicide squad " employed as escorts against
surface raiders in the western ocean.[1] She had just completed
an east-bound convoy trip and was due to return to Halifax.
Baker-Cresswell offered Pawsey the " Hobson's choice " of
joining his next convoy instead of proceeding west independently through the danger area, or of accepting the only escort
available for him, which would be two slow trawlers; and the
A.M.C. Captain unhesitatingly accepted the offer to join the
convoy. Plans for the next outward movement from Iceland
could now be finalised between the Naval Officer in Charge
(Rear-Admiral R. J. R. Scott), his R.A.F. colleague of No. 15
Group (Group Captain W. H. Primrose) and the senior officer
of the escorts.

[1] See p. 56.

On the evening of 6th May the four merchantmen from Iceland[1] which were to join OB.318 sailed under the escort of the corvettes *Aubrietia*, *Hollyhock* and *Nigella*, and the trawler *St. Apollo*, all of the 3rd Escort Group; and the movement was duly reported to all concerned by the Naval Control Service Officer in Iceland. At 2.15 next morning Baker-Cresswell, with the *Bulldog*, *Amazon* and *Broadway* (the three available destroyers of his group) took the old *Ranpura* under his wing and set course to find his convoy. The A.M.C. certainly had an ample and comforting escort for the first leg of her westward journey; but her Captain's peace of mind was not to stay undisturbed for long. The trawler *Daneman* was delayed by a boiler defect, and did not get away with the rest of the group. She joined the convoy, however, at a critical moment next evening.

Baker-Cresswell knew that, with his three corvettes astern of him escorting the merchantmen from Iceland, and all his three trawlers temporarily absent, he was going to be very short-handed to begin with; but his first problem was to find the convoy. He knew from the signals he had received that the enemy was in touch, and that it had been diverted from its original course; and this was likely to make it harder to find, because alterations of course were bound to delay a convoy, and they did not, moreover, always adhere strictly to the courses ordered. Commodores of convoys always had discretion to act on their own initiative in such matters, in consultation with the escort commander. The 3rd Escort Group reached the rendezvous with time in hand; but the visibility was poor, with patches of mist, and Baker-Cresswell cannot have been surprised that there was no sign of the merchantmen. As so often he had an awkward moment before deciding in which direction to search; but his first cast again proved

[1] These merchantmen were the *Cardium* (Brit. tanker, 8,236 tons), the *Bradglen* (Brit. 4,741 tons), the *Borgfred* (Norw. 2,183 tons) and the *Gunvor Maersk* (Dan. 1,977 tons).

lucky and at 5.45 p.m. he sighted the merchantmen under Bockett-Pugh's charge in 61°14 North 23°37 West. This was actually 15 minutes early on the planned time, and only 7 miles north of the planned position of the rendezvous[1]— which was a good deal better in both respects than was often accomplished; but OB.318 had so far had favourable weather. The two group commanders now brought their ships close together, transferred the relevant orders from the *Westcott* to the *Bulldog* and held a short conference over their loud-hailers. Bockett-Pugh's destroyers (the *Westcott*, *Newmarket* and *Campbeltown*) had none too much fuel remaining, and they would have to leave the convoy that evening; but he agreed to leave all the rest of his group (the sloop *Rochester*, the corvettes *Nasturtium*, *Aubrietia*, *Dianthus*, *Primrose* and *Marigold*) to continue with the convoy under Baker-Cresswell's orders for a further 24 hours. On the evening of 8th May they would have to be detached in order to meet the fast east-bound convoy HX.123 as ordered by Admiral Noble. At 7.45 p.m. Baker-Cresswell took over responsibility for OB.318 and the destroyers of the 7th Escort Group left for Hvalfiord soon afterwards. In his report on the convoy Bockett-Pugh said that it was " well handled, organised and disciplined " and that " station keeping had been noticeably good." He had, however, severely censured the *Burma*, the Rear-Commodore's ship, for showing a bright light.

Baker-Cresswell now had his own three destroyers and six of Bockett-Pugh's ships. He left the latter in the screening positions which they already occupied, stationed the *Amazon* (Lieutenant-Commander N. E. G. Roper) ahead of the port columns, his own *Bulldog* ahead of the starboard columns, and the *Broadway* (Lieutenant-Commander T. Taylor) astern of the port columns. The A.M.C. *Ranpura* he placed in the centre of the convoy, whose fifth and sixth columns opened out to make room for her. There she stood out, as Baker-Cresswell

[1] See p. 61.

remarked, like a haystack. The formation of the convoy at this time, on its mean course of N. 42° W. (true) is shown below; but the escorts were of course zig-zagging independently.

The first sign of danger came little more than an hour after Baker-Cresswell had taken over the convoy; for just before 9 p.m. his *Bulldog* gained Asdic contact with some object 200 yards ahead of her. The contact was, however, lost before it could be classified, so Baker-Cresswell reversed course and

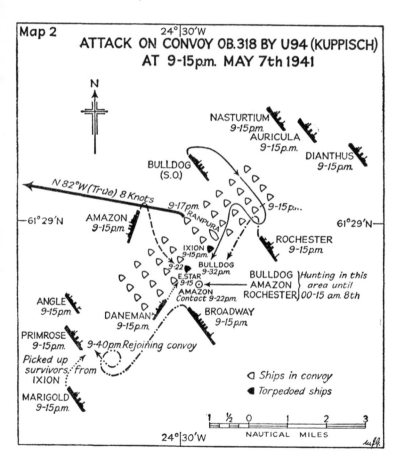

Map 2

24° 30′ W

ATTACK ON CONVOY OB.318 BY U94 (KUPPISCH) AT 9-15 p.m. MAY 7th 1941

N

NASTURTIUM
9-15 p.m.

AURICULA
9-15 p.m.

DIANTHUS
9-15 p.m.

BULLDOG
(S.O.)

N 82° W (True) 8 Knots

9-17 p.m.

RANPURA

9-15 p.m.

—61° 29′ N

AMAZON
9-15 p.m.

61° 29′ N—

ROCHESTER
9-15 p.m.

IXION
9-15 p.m.

9-22

BULLDOG
9-32 p.m.

E.STAR
9-15

BULLDOG } Hunting in this
AMAZON } area until
ROCHESTER } 00-15 am. 8th

AMAZON
Contact 9-22 p.m.

ANGLE
9-15 p.m.

DANEMAN
9-15 p.m.

BROADWAY
9-15 p.m.

PRIMROSE
9-15 p.m.

9-40 p.m. Rejoining convoy

Picked up
survivors from
IXION

▷ Ships in convoy
◀ Torpedoed ships

MARIGOLD
9-15 p.m.

1 ½ 0   1   2   3
NAUTICAL   MILES

24° 30′ W

passed down through the convoy between the seventh and eighth columns. Nothing more had been heard when, at 9.15, the fourth ship in column 4 (the *Eastern Star*) and the fourth in column 5 (the *Ixion*) were torpedoed almost simultaneously. The *Bulldog* was actually inside the convoy at the time, about abreast of the rear ships, and Baker-Cresswell at once realised that the torpedoes must have been fired from a position very near to his ship or the *Rochester*.[1] He dropped one depth charge and told the *Rochester* to do the same; but neither ship obtained any sign of a contact. He also told the trawler *Daneman*, which had just joined the convoy from Iceland and had been stationed in the rear of the convoy between Columns 1 and 2, to stand by the *Eastern Star*, which had caught fire and was blazing furiously, and the corvette *Marigold* to do the same for the *Ixion*. Within two minutes of the attack Commodore Mackenzie had turned the convoy 40 degrees to port by emergency signal. This produced some hectic moments for the *Bulldog*, which was still inside the convoy, and found herself surrounded by manœuvring merchantmen. Meanwhile the *Amazon* was coming down through the convoy, and the senior officer ordered her to join the *Rochester* for a counter-attack, while the *Broadway* searched on the port quarter. When the *Broadway* had swept out to a distance of two miles without finding anything Baker-Cresswell ordered Taylor to rejoin the convoy and take charge of it; for the escort had of course been much depleted by these movements. A few minutes later Lieutenant-Commander C. B. Allen of the *Rochester* received a report from an alert look-out on his quarter-deck " Periscope in sight on the port beam." He could not see it himself from the bridge, but almost simultaneously Lieutenant-Commander Roper's *Amazon* gained contact at 1,700 yards. He quickly manœuvred astern of the *Daneman*, which was picking up the *Eastern Star*'s crew, and at 9.26 fired a full pattern of ten depth charges with deep (150–350 feet) settings, followed

[1] See Map 2 (p. 87).

by a second one nine minutes later, for which, however, only five charges (set to 150 feet) were ready. The *Rochester* had now also gained contact, and it was she who attacked next, with a full pattern, at 9.41. Meanwhile Baker-Cresswell had extricated his *Bulldog* from the convoy, and came across to join in the hunt. The *Bulldog* and *Amazon* had trained together as the 3rd Escort Group's Striking Force, but Baker-Cresswell kept Allen's *Rochester* with him as she was also in contact with the U-boat. The safety of the *Ranpura*, which he had more or less invited to come along with him, was not the least of the escort commander's anxieties at this time, and he signalled to ask how her Captain now felt about his decision. Pawsey replied, however, that he still considered he had done rightly.

At 9.48 the *Bulldog* was also in contact, and came in with her first full pattern, which was soon followed by others from the *Amazon* and the *Rochester*. Thus did 55 depth charges, released in six separate and deliberate attacks, rain down upon the U-boat within little more than half-an-hour of the first contact; but Asdic conditions were none too good, and although the attackers believed that they had damaged the enemy, and were hopeful of finishing him off, they realised that they were up against a skilful and wily antagonist. Between 10 and 10.30 p.m. all three ships regained contact, only to lose it again; but at 10.30 the *Rochester* and *Amazon* were once more firmly on to the enemy, and the latter carried out her fourth attack with the *Rochester* directing her movements. Roper considered this to have been his most accurate pattern so far. As the plume from the ten depth charges subsided a large bubble of air came to the surface. The *Rochester*, however, maintained contact, and just as Roper was about to come in for his fifth attack the U-boat altered course making straight for the *Rochester* at high speed! This was a cunning manœuvre, for it forced Roper to break off his attack while the enemy passed under Allen's ship; but the two ships' Asdic operators both held the U-boat, and the *Amazon* got in her delayed attack soon afterwards. Roper was now running short of depth charges, and rationed himself to five in each subsequent pattern. The *Bulldog*, however, got in another full pattern at 11.20, and ten minutes later Roper made his sixth and final attack. Again the target swung rapidly to starboard as he moved in, and the British ships realised that their enemy was not only adept at evading their onslaught, but had probably not yet suffered serious damage.

Soon after midnight the contact seemed to have faded for good, and Baker-Cresswell ordered the *Rochester* back to the convoy. He and the *Amazon*, however, continued the search throughout the rest of the night, and not until 9.30 a.m. on the 8th did they abandon the pursuit and set course to catch up the convoy.

To return to the torpedoed merchantmen, it was a curious coincidence that both the *Eastern Star* and the *Ixion* seem to have been carrying large quantities of whisky in their holds. The former caught fire at once, and was soon a mass of flames. Baker-Cresswell, glancing at the cargo list at the moment she was struck, thought regretfully of the sad waste of a commodity which was then so strictly rationed in Britain. The *Nailsea Manor* (No. 94 in the convoy), which had been detailed as rescue ship, at once turned back to assist her stricken comrades, and both Baker-Cresswell and Commodore Mackenzie commended her Master for his promptitude. The *Nailsea Manor* belonged to the Nailsea Steamship Company of Cardiff; but they sold their last ship in 1949, and it has thus proved impossible to trace the name of the ship's Master at the time of this incident. In some reports on convoy OB.318 the ship is referred to as the *Nailsea Moor*, and it is a fact that the company then also owned a ship of that name of identical tonnage to the *Nailsea Manor*. On balance, however, it seems probable that it was the *Nailsea Manor* which sailed in OB.318.

When the *Ixion* was struck her Master, Captain W. F. Dark, acted with exemplary calm. He fired rockets, threw his confidential books overboard in a weighted bag, and ordered his crew of 105 officers and men to their boat stations. He even had time to note that " a strong smell of whisky was coming from the hold where the ship had been hit." Next he asked the Engine Room for a report on the ship's condition, and received from his imperturbable Chief Engineer the answer that " she was all right in a way, but bulkheads were leaking and there was 6 inches of water on the plates." Dark thereupon went down below himself to see how matters really stood, and on finding the engine room nearly flooded he gave the order to " abandon ship." Five boatloads with 86 survivors were picked up by the *Nailsea Manor*; while Dark and his Chief Officer, who had left the ship in " the small boat " with 17 others, were rescued by the corvette *Marigold* (Lieutenant James Renwick, R.N.R.). Not a man was lost, and Dark himself at once suggested that, as they were only about 80 miles from Reykjavik, a tug should be called to tow the *Ixion* in. Plainly he was determined that his fine ship should, if possible, be saved.

The rescue of the *Eastern Star*'s crew was a far more difficult undertaking, for she became a roaring furnace so quickly that no ship could approach near her. From the *Bulldog* Baker-Cresswell could see men jumping overboard, and he feared that the casualty list would be heavy. But the trawler *Daneman* (Lieutenant A. H. Ballard, R.N.R.) closed as near as she dared to the burning wreck, and soon reported that she had not only rescued Mr. Olav Østervold[1], the Master of the ship, and the whole of his crew, but was busily engaged in salvaging cases of Vat 69. Doubtless the contents were issued as " medical comforts " to the merchantman's survivors and her own company when, on the completion of a very gallant effort, she set course to rejoin the convoy at 10.30 p.m.

[1] Until shortly before the *Eastern Star* sailed on her last voyage Mr. Olav Østervold was Chief Officer of the ship, and his father, Mr. Jan Østervold, was the Master.

The *Eastern Star* sank at about 1.15 a.m. next morning; but hopes of saving the *Ixion* appeared good, and a signal was sent to Reykjavik for a tug. Her bulkheads must, however, have given way; for about $1\frac{1}{2}$ hours after the blazing hulk of the *Eastern Star* had disappeared, she suddenly sank by the stern. Nine hundred bags of mail, some of them diplomatic bags, went down with her. The *Marigold*, which had been standing by her, then set course to rejoin the convoy, and overtook it at noon on 8th. She finally landed Captain Dark and his boat's crew at Greenock, while the rest of the *Ixion*'s company were carried on to Canada in the *Nailsea Manor*.

There was no doubt that the first round of the contest between OB.318's escort and the U-boats had gone to the latter. We now know that Kapitänleutnant Kuppisch of U.94 sighted the convoy's funnel smoke at 6.05 p.m., assessed its mean course as North 15° West (true) and its speed as 9 knots (in both of which his observations were fairly accurate) and took station ahead of it. The reader will remark that Kuppisch's sighting took place just after the 3rd Escort Group had first contacted the convoy; and it may well be that his success owed a good deal to the lucky chance of meeting the convoy just when the escorts were changing over. At 7.06 the U-boat Commander signalled to his headquarters that he was in touch, and was told to attack if possible, but in any case to continue shadowing the convoy. For some unexplained reason U.94's first sighting report seems to have been missed by the Admiralty's listening stations.

Kuppisch lost no time in carrying out the order to attack. At 7.54, while still well ahead of the convoy, he dived in order to keep out of sight. " I planned," he wrote in his log, " to get right inside the convoy in order to be able to fire to all sides from all torpedo tubes." He took several quick looks through his periscope, but the sea was so smooth that, to avoid betraying his presence, he could only use it very sparingly. As he closed the convoy a destroyer (probably Baker-Cresswell's own

Bulldog) was seen approaching, and he went deep. It seems almost certain that the *Bulldog*'s brief contact at 8.58 actually was on U.94; but Kuppisch had by that time almost achieved his object of obscuring his presence in the wakes of the many merchantmen. He probably entered the convoy in the big space between columns 5 and 6, where the *Ranpura* was stationed[1]; and at his next peep through the periscope he saw that a zig-zag had placed him " between two 10,000-ton liners "—presumably the *Ranpura* and the *Ixion*. He was in a perfect firing position, and between 9.09–50 and 9.11–50 he fired three single shots from his bow tubes at " large merchant-men," and one from his stern tubes " at a tanker." The latter target must have been either the *El Mirlo* or *Lucerna* in Column 5. Kuppisch said that he heard loud explosions at the end of each torpedo's running time; but in fact the stern shot must have missed. At least two of the torpedoes fired from the bow tubes, however, found their marks—though we cannot say whether the ships Kuppisch hit were those he had actually aimed at. From such a favourable attacking position a torpedo which missed one ship might very well hit another. On balance it seems likely that the *Ixion* was struck by one torpedo and the *Eastern Star* by two, and that those which destroyed the latter ship were actually aimed at Captain Pawsey's *Ranpura*. It is hard to believe that such a luscious target as the big A.M.C. would not have attracted at any rate part of the U-boat commander's salvo.

At 9.20 p.m. Kuppisch brought U.94 up to periscope depth again, to take a look at the damage he had accomplished: and that action led, as we have seen, to the long hunt by the *Bulldog*, *Amazon* and *Rochester*. In his report Kuppisch said that he was " subjected to a very severe and accurate counter-attack, which lasted for four hours and caused considerable damage."

In one attack, probably the *Amazon*'s fourth at 10.36 p.m., the depth charge pattern exploded right above the U-boat.

[1] See Diagram 3 (back end paper).

Evidently the charges had not been set quite deep enough to do lethal damage. Kuppisch counted 67 depth charges, but our ships' records show that, including the four dropped by *Bulldog* and *Broadway* before firm contact was gained, 89 was the actual total released. No doubt some of them exploded so nearly simultaneously that Kuppisch counted them as one charge.

U.94 suffered temporary damage to her after hydroplanes; her engine room telegraphs and magnetic compass, and also her gyro repeaters were put out of action; a number of gauges were shattered and some of her compressed air bottles started to leak. But her captain never lost his nerve. It is plain that at several critical moments he judged the movements of his assailants to a nicety, and manœuvred out of the way of their depth charges very skilfully. The damage he sustained, though serious enough to prevent him joining in the pursuit of OB.318, did not force him to abandon his patrol. He continued at sea, firstly off Greenland and then off western Ireland for a total of 37 days, and finally arrived at St. Nazaire on 4th June. He claimed to have sunk 6 ships totalling 32,128 tons during his cruise—four of them (20,000 tons) in the attack on OB.318. In fact, as we have seen, he only sank two ships totalling 15,901 tons on 7th May. The Germans had picked up the emergency signals sent by the *Ixion* and *Eastern Star* when they were torpedoed; but they none the less credited Kuppisch with the full results which he claimed—an example of how they so commonly misled themselves regarding their own achievements. None the less Kuppisch certainly deserved the commendation which Dönitz awarded him for his attack on 7th May. "This," said the Commander of the U-boats, "was a very good operation, tenaciously and successfully carried out." We for our part assessed the counter-attacks against U.94 as having "probably damaged" her; which, as we have seen, was very near the truth.

Travelling in the Rear-Commodore's ship, the S.S. *Burma*,

were over 100 passengers bound for South Africa and the Middle East. Among them was a very observant clergyman of the Church of England, the Reverend R. Ashley Long-botham[1], then aged 26, who was travelling to Durban to join the staff of St. Paul's Church in that town. It was his first long sea voyage, and during it he kept a diary which, with an appropriately nautical touch, he called his "log." In it he gives such a vivid description of how the events described in this book appeared at the time to a newcomer to the sea and a stranger to the perils of wartime convoy passages, that permission was sought, and readily granted, to quote from it.

Sunday, 4th May, 1941

We are steaming due north through the Minches, between the mainland of Scotland and the Hebrides. Most of us were astonished to see land on either side when we came on deck this morning. I served at Holy Communion at 7 a.m., and after boat drill at 10 a.m. we held Divine Service in the music room.[2] The Naval Chaplain, Worrel, officiated and gave a good address "Ambassador of Jesus Christ," and a Dutchman played the piano for four well-known hymns. The convoy has now formed up in seven or eight parallel lines, and three destroyers and about three corvettes are escorting us. At regular intervals planes circle overhead. At 6 p.m., off Cape Wrath, we turned west and began to steam out into the Atlantic.

Monday, 5th May

We are now getting out into the ocean, in a very northerly latitude, probably about 60° North. We· have steamed 201 miles between noon yesterday and noon to-day. The convoy has kept in the formation adopted yesterday evening,

[1] Now (1958) Vicar of Aldingbourne, nr. Chichester.
[2] The times given in this diary are, of course, the local times kept in the convoy. In the rest of this book all times (British and German) have been adjusted to Greenwich Mean Time.

and planes still continue to circle the ships at regular intervals. This is comforting, and gives a sense of fair security. We are still at the beginning of a long, tedious and somewhat dangerous voyage, and we are entering the most perilous region. The ocean is big, pitiless and deep, but God is good and his mercy is great.

Tuesday, 6th May

Escorting planes still coming out to us, but later in the day they leave us on our own. A Sunderland flying boat paid us a visit at about tea-time. There is nothing much to report. Sea still calm, and we steamed 202 miles in the last 24 hours. I *nearly* won a game of chess against Maurice James (another young chaplain) to-night.

Wednesday, 7th May

To-day will live long in our memories. The weather was exceptionally fine. Even the Captain remarked that not in his long life had he known the Atlantic so calm so far to the north. But in spite of the brilliant sky evil things were at hand. A signal for " Action Stations " came at about noon, the Commodore sounding his siren and other ships following suit. Three destroyers, two corvettes and a Sunderland flying-boat went off to the south-east, and we heard depth charges being dropped. This caused some excitement, but passengers and crew were very calm. The convoy turned north, and after half an hour wheeled back to its proper course, zig-zagging as it went. The " All Clear " was given at about 1.30 and most of us went to the dining-saloon for lunch. It was good and comforting to see the Captain at his table eating a hearty meal !

We then steamed steadily West by North. The weather was without blemish. At 7.30 p.m. I went to my cabin to say my evening prayers. I specially prayed that God would bless this convoy with his Almighty protection. No sooner had I risen from my knees and gone on deck than I saw that a big armed merchant cruiser and several more escorts had joined. It seemed as though this was in direct answer to my prayers; but the devil's will was otherwise. Feeling tired I went to my cabin and turned in at 10 p.m., and at about 11.15 heard two distinct explosions. I got out of my bunk, put on my life-jacket and my heavy coat, and went on deck. A terrible sight met my eyes. Two ships in our convoy, not quarter of a mile away, had been struck by torpedoes. One of them was on fire, with a terrible volume of black smoke pouring from her, and the other was listing heavily. For a second my mind went blank, but things were happening near at hand, where a U-boat was lurking, and I felt as though we were now truly in the Battle of the Atlantic. I could see one boat leave the burning ship— thank goodness there were some survivors. Our convoy immediately took a right-angle turn to starboard, destroyers raced to the spot where the U-boat was thought to be, and ship-shaking depth charges were dropped. I felt sorry for the U-boat, but this ghastly ship-sinking business is nothing but sheer cold-blooded murder. Our ship's company and passengers, standing by the lifeboats, were splendidly steadfast. By midnight both ships could be seen well down in the water. One of the rear ships of the convoy acted as rescue ship, and picked up survivors—at least that is what we hoped. I offered prayers for the souls of the departed. By 1 a.m. things were quieter, escort vessels were signalling by flashlight, and the convoy was back into its normal night routine. We were very fortunate to escape in our first U-boat attack. However brightly the sun may have shone earlier the day ended terribly for us all. Sleep did not come until 4 a.m. Mileage from noon to noon 198.

CHAPTER VII

The Second Attack, 9th May

At 10 p.m. on the 7th, only about an hour after U.94 had torpedoed the *Ixion* and *Eastern Star*, the corvettes *Aubrietia* (Lieutenant-Commander V. F. Smith, R.N.R.), *Nigella* (Lieutenant T. W. Coyne, R.N.R.), and *Hollyhock* (Lieutenant T. E. Davies, R.N.R.), and the trawler *St. Apollo* (Lieutenant R. H. Marchington, R.N.V.R.) joined the convoy with the four west-bound merchantmen from Iceland. The Commodore had just resumed his north-westerly course after making the emergency turn to port, and the newly arrived merchantmen promptly took up the vacant stations in the convoy. There was now an exceptionally powerful escort available; for the 3rd Escort Group's nine ships had all joined up, and the 7th Escort Group's four corvettes were still with the convoy. But as the *Bulldog*, *Amazon* and *Rochester* were still hunting U.94 well astern of the convoy, it would be some time before all ships had concentrated again for its defence. Lieutenant-Commander T. Taylor in the *Broadway* took command of the escort until Baker-Cresswell rejoined with his *Bulldog*; but that did not happen until the following afternoon.

At 11.35 p.m. on the 7th, by which time the convoy had reached latitude 62° North, Commodore Mackenzie altered to a due westerly course in accordance with the order passed by the Admiralty earlier that day.[1] The reason was that the Submarine Tracking Room apparently thought that another U-boat might be lurking further to the north. The night passed quietly, however, and at 7 a.m. the *Broadway* signalled

[1] See p. 79.

the convoy's position and its new course. The message was picked up in Britain and re-broadcast by Admiral Noble, so that the detached escorts should know where to look for the merchantmen. At 8.30 another of No. 204 Squadron's Sunderlands from Iceland joined up to give close escort until early in the afternoon, when the renewed threat of fog at its base caused its recall. Meanwhile other Sunderlands were sweeping to the south-west of Iceland; but they sighted no enemies. This was the last occasion on which air escort was provided for OB.318.

On rejoining the convoy at 4 p.m. on 8th Baker-Cresswell released the 7th Escort Group's four corvettes (the *Dianthus*, *Nasturtium*, *Primrose*, and *Auricula*), which were due to make for a rendezvous with the homeward convoy HX.123, with his grateful thanks for their help. He now had his own three destroyers, three corvettes, and three trawlers, and decided to adopt his favourite day screening disposition. Ahead of the convoy, from left to right, he stationed the *Amazon*, *Hollyhock*, *Bulldog*, *Nigella* and *Broadway*. The trawler *Angle* and the corvette *Aubrietia* he tucked into the port and starboard wing columns, so that if a U-boat penetrated the screen ahead and attacked from either beam they would be well placed to deal with it; and the trawlers *Daneman* and *St. Apollo* he stationed astern to round up stragglers and look after any ship that got into difficulties. He felt confident that he had shaken off, and perhaps damaged the assailant of the previous night, and as no more warnings had come through from the Admiralty he had no reason to foresee further trouble. At 8.45 p.m. the convoy reached the position on the course laid down by the Admiralty where it was to turn from a westerly to a south-westerly course[1], and the Commodore therefore altered to South 30° West (true). It was now about 300 miles to the south-west of Reykjavik in Iceland.

Dusk fell at about 10.30 p.m., and in accordance with his

[1] See Map 1 (front end paper).

usual custom Baker-Cresswell sent off the *Amazon* and *Broadway* to search out to ten miles on either beam of the convoy; but they sighted nothing, and soon returned to their night screening positions. Meanwhile the 7th Escort Group's four corvettes were carrying out an extensive search astern of the convoy, before making for their new rendezvous. As an additional precaution, at 11.45 p.m. Commodore Mackenzie made an evasive 30-degree turn to starboard; and by midnight the 3rd Escort Group had settled down to what seemed likely to prove yet another night's watchful screening, with little to disturb the peace except the continuous " pinging " of their Asdics and the periodic rings of the zig-zag clocks.

But U-boat Headquarters had not yet finished with OB.318, and on the 8th Dönitz wrote in his War Diary that he was moving the northern boats further west " for the reasons set out on 6th May " (*i.e.*, to take advantage of the greater spread of our shipping between 25° and 30° West[1]). Six boats were immediately affected (U.94, U.556, U.201, U.97, U.93 and U.98); but another one, U.110, had meanwhile arrived south of Iceland from France, and as she concerns us very intimately we will follow her history in some detail.

Her Commanding Officer was Kapitänleutnant Fritz-Julius Lemp, who was the son of an army officer and was born in the Germany colony of Tsingtao (China) in February, 1913. He had joined the Navy early in 1931, and achieved his first command seven years later. Although we did not know it until after the war Lemp had achieved a high degree of notoriety as Captain of U.30 by sinking the Donaldson liner *Athenia* with heavy loss of life on the very day that war was declared. Even in German circles that act caused some consternation, for it directly contravened Hitler's orders that the U-boats were to wage war only in accordance with the Hague Conventions. Hitler's reasoning was not altruistic. He wished only to avoid a repetition of the consequences of

[1] See p. 73.

sinking ships such as the *Lusitania* in the 1914–18 war. Lemp's actions were fully investigated, and he was held to have mistaken the *Athenia* for a troopship, and to have " acted in good faith "; but the Germans decided to hush the whole matter up, the incriminating pages were removed from U.30's log and destroyed, and the whole truth did not come out until the trials of the major " war criminals " took place at Nuremberg. The circumstances in which the *Athenia* was sunk, and the actions taken to conceal the identity of the culprit were then produced as evidence in support of the charges against Dönitz. On the British side the consequences of Lemp's action against the *Athenia* were by no means wholly unfortunate; for it convinced us that the Germans intended at once to resume unrestricted U-boat warfare against merchantmen, and so eliminated our last lingering doubts regarding the need to sail ships in convoy.

Lemp made no less than eight war cruises in U.30, but only three of them yielded any significant results. It was he who, on 28th December, 1939, hit the battleship *Barham* with one torpedo, and on arriving back in Germany from his eighth sortie in August, 1940, he found himself a hero with nine merchantmen alleged to total 46,500 tons to his credit. Though his actual sinkings, including the *Athenia*, amounted to only six ships (31,648 tons), he was entertained by Dönitz and awarded the Knight's Insignia of the Iron Cross.

On 21st November, 1940, Lemp commissioned the new Type IXB boat U.110 at Bremen. She was a 1,050-ton " Atlantic boat," of a class which gave the enemy excellent service in the more distant waters. Her " legend " was as follows:—

LENGTH:	252.5 feet.
BEAM:	22.3 feet.
DRAUGHT (*laden*):	15.5 feet.
DISPLACEMENTS:	1,050 tons surfaced.
	1,178 tons submerged.

MAXIMUM SPEED: 18.2 knots (on surface).
                  7.3 knots (submerged).
ENDURANCE: 12,400 miles at 10 knots, on diesel-electric
                  drive.
                  64 miles at 4 knots submerged, on electric
                  motors.
DIVING DEPTH: 330 feet.
ARMAMENTS: 4 bow, 2 stern torpedo tubes; 19 torpedoes
                  carried or, alternatively, 44–66 mines
                  (depending on type).
                  1–10.5 cm. (4.2 inch) quick-firing gun.
                  1–37 mm. and 2–20 mm. A.A. guns.

Lemp took with him to U.110 three officers who had served
with him in U.30 (Oberleutnants-zur-See, Greger and Loewe,
and Leutnant Wehrhofer), and in November, 1940, the new
boat sailed for the Baltic to carry out trials. She was, however,
delayed by defects which developed in her diesels and her
electric motors, and it was 9th March, 1941, before she was
ready to sail on her first war cruise. The middle of that month
saw the " wolf pack " attack on convoy HX.112 in which
U.99 (Kretschmer) and U.100 (Schepke) were sunk.[1] Lemp's
U.110 was also involved in that operation. He sank the 6,207-
ton tanker *Erodona* on 15th March, and was then hunted by
the *Volunteer* and *Vanoc*; but he got away, and took no part
in the next night's attacks when his two distinguished colleagues
lost their ships. On 23rd March Lemp pursued a small
Norwegian ship and engaged her with his guns; but one of the
crew evidently forgot to remove the gun's muzzle tampion
before firing (an omission which has also been known in the
Royal Navy!), the gun exploded and the boat's periscope
was damaged. Lemp had to abandon his cruise, and arrived
in Lorient on 29th. He considered that his young crew had,
with few exceptions, done well on their first war operation,

[1] See p. 51.

and that they were now " efficient and blooded." Dönitz visited the ship soon after her arrival in port, and awarded several Iron Crosses. He seems to have had a soft spot for Lemp, and wrote on his report that he agreed with all the Captain's remarks and actions—except regarding the forgotten gun tampion! There is no doubt at all that Lemp was a very popular as well as an efficient Commanding Officer; for his crew later described him as " well liked, even-tempered, very determined, and possessed of unshakable calm "; but while at Lorient after U.110's first cruise Oberleutnant Dietrich Loewe relieved Greger as First Lieutenant; and he was evidently a very different type of man.

Though a cousin of Lemp, who was certainly not the man to tolerate discord in his ship or inefficiency among his crew, Loewe was apparently not popular with the men, who held him in small regard. Moreover German sailors (like British ones) are evidently superstitious; and the fact that two of the ships in which Loewe had previously served had been sunk made them regard him as something of a " Jonah." He was, moreover, an ardent Nazi, and seems to have behaved callously towards his subordinates. To make matters worse the junior executive officer, Leutnant-zur-See Ulrich Wehrhofer, was regarded as unreliable. If indeed one accepts the contemporary views of their shipmates regarding those two officers it is difficult to avoid the conclusion that Lemp himself must have been a poor judge of character. On the other hand the Engineer Officer, Leutnant Hans-Joachim Eichelborn, had a pleasant personality and was considered very competent at his job. The Petty Officers were nearly all experienced men, who had served some time with Lemp. One of them, who had formerly been an officer in the Merchant Navy, had been shockingly treated in a concentration camp—presumably because of his political views. In marked contrast to the senior ratings, many of the younger men were still very raw and inexperienced; and, in spite of the Captain's optimism, those who had watched their reactions during the first cruise had serious doubts regarding their ability to face a serious emergency without panicking. The total complement was four officers (Lemp, Loewe, Wehrhofer and Eichelborn), fifteen Petty Officers and 27 junior ratings—46 in all; but before leaving Lorient a war correspondent, Helmuth Ecke, also embarked for the cruise.

U.110 sailed outward-bound on 15th April, and five days later was on patrol to the west of Ireland. Nothing happened until 26th, when she sighted a steamer; and late that night Lemp sank her. She turned out to be the Vichy French ship *André Moyrand*. Once again Lemp had aimed his torpedoes at an ill-chosen target. He next began to move west on the surface, and made good progress until, early on 8th May, an aircraft forced him to dive. This was probably one of No. 204 Squadron's Sunderlands, which were then searching to the south-west of Iceland. That afternoon Lemp brought U.110 to the surface again, and at 4 p.m. he sighted smoke ahead. There is no doubt at all that it came from convoy OB.318. Lemp's report reached U-boat Headquarters some two hours later, and he was told to attack if possible, but in any event to shadow the convoy. Dönitz also ordered the other boats in the vicinity to report their positions, so that their attacks could be co-ordinated. But the listeners at the British wireless stations had also picked up Lemp's sighting report, and at 7.07 p.m. the Admiralty signalled a warning that they considered OB.318 was still being shadowed. This time their deduction was perfectly correct; but the message shattered the hope, which had been rising in the convoy since the previous midnight, that the alteration of course to the west had shaken off all pursuers. At dusk, therefore, Commodore Mackenzie made an evasive alteration of 30° to port; but it is in fact almost impossible for an 8-knot convoy to rid itself of a determined shadower by such means—especially on a fine, moonlit night.

After it had become dark Lemp closed in cautiously with

the intention of attacking; but he found the bright moonlight little to his liking, and even though none of the escorts detected him he was evidently aware that they were present in considerable strength. He decided that discretion was the better policy, and withdrew again to continue shadowing from the starboard beam or quarter. At 4.16 a.m. on 9th he again reported the convoy's position and course, and soon afterwards Dönitz's attempts to concentrate several U-boats against it bore fruit. U.201 (Oberleutnant-zur-See Adelbert Schnee) had intercepted Lemp's earlier sighting report, and had been working round to the north of convoy during the night. He actually sighted OB.318 at 8.30 a.m., and soon afterwards gained visual touch with Lemp. The two captains brought their boats close together, and discussed their mode of attack. Their decision was that Lemp should go first, and that Schnee would follow after half an hour's interval. They believed that U.556 (Kapitänleutnant Herbert Wohlfarth), whom we shall encounter again shortly, and possibly U.96 and U.553 were also in the vicinity; but as no other boats had made their presence known Lemp and Schnee decided to delay no longer. Actually U.556 was still some way to the east at the time, and neither of the other two U-boats was anywhere near the scene. In retrospect, however, it does seem rather unlucky, from the British point of view, that this conference between two surfaced U-boats should have taken place just out of sight of the convoy at the very moment when our air escorts had ceased. Baker-Cresswell and his consorts were, of course, completely unaware of what was being hatched just over the wide rim of the northern horizon.

After a comparatively undisturbed night on the charthouse settee Baker-Cresswell came on to the *Bulldog*'s bridge at about 4.30 a.m. on the 9th to watch his group take up their day screening positions. This was to be the last day with the convoy, and when his ships' fuel reports came in the escort commander knew that they would have to break off at about

4 p.m. if they were to reach Iceland with a reasonable margin. By that time it should be perfectly safe to disperse the convoy; for no U-boat had yet attacked so far to the west. In spite of the Admiralty's warning of the previous evening the situation seemed quite satisfactory, and the pleasant train of thought passing through the commander's mind was soon enhanced by the sight of his unfailing steward Gaston dodging along the upper deck between waves with his breakfast wrapped in a napkin.

The forenoon passed quietly on a course of South 40° West (true), Baker-Cresswell took his sun sights and was just preparing to exchange noon positions with the Commodore when, suddenly, a column of water shot up on the starboard side of the *Esmond* (No. 91), the leader of the starboard wing column.[1] A few seconds later it was followed by a rumbling explosion. She had been hit by two torpedoes. For a second or two Baker-Cresswell stared incredulously; since a torpedo attack in longitude 33° West, almost within sight of the Greenland coast, seemed highly improbable. But hardly had the thought come and passed when the *Bengore Head* (No. 71), the leader of Column 7, was also struck. Lieutenant-Commander Dodds, Chief Engineer of the *Bulldog*, happened to be on deck at the time, and he saw the *Esmond's* stern lift out of the water and rise steadily upwards to the vertical, while her deck cargo of vehicles and cased goods from her holds cascaded into the sea, reminding him " of a child pouring toys out of a box." Then she slid slowly and steadily beneath the surface, until only bubbles remained to mark her grave. The *Bengore Head* was hit amidships and broke her back immediately, but her bow and stern remained afloat for some time with the two masts actually crossing.

As soon as the first torpedo exploded the Commodore ordered an emergency turn to port, and Baker-Cresswell, realising that the attack must have come from between the

[1] See Map 3. (opposite).

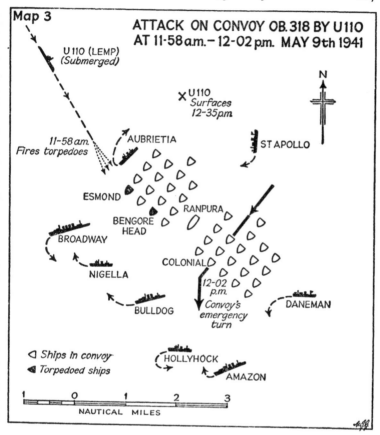

Map 3

ATTACK ON CONVOY OB. 318 BY U 110
AT 11·58 a.m. – 12·02 pm. MAY 9th 1941

U 110 (LEMP)
(Submerged)

U 110
Surfaces
12·35 pm

N

11·58 am.
Fires torpedoes

AUBRIETIA

ST APOLLO

ESMOND

RANPURA

BENGORE
HEAD

BROADWAY

NIGELLA

COLONIAL

12·02
p.m.

BULLDOG

DANEMAN

Convoy's
emergency
turn

◁ Ships in convoy
◀ Torpedoed ships

HOLLYHOCK

AMAZON

0   1   2   3
1
NAUTICAL   MILES

Broadway and *Aubrietia*, reacted instinctively. Telling Roper of the *Amazon* to take charge of the convoy he swung the *Bulldog* round towards the position from which the U-boat must have fired. Taylor did much the same manœuvre with his *Broadway*; but it was not the destroyers which located the enemy first this time.

We cannot be quite certain with regard to the course of events on board U.110 after she parted from U.201, but Lemp seems to have acted with a degree of confidence amounting almost to recklessness. Some of his officers urged him to postpone the attack for a few hours, as they realised, quite correctly, that the powerful escort must soon leave the convoy; but Lemp did not wish to be drawn too far to the west. He dived at 10.37 a.m. and approached the convoy from the starboard bow. At one minute before noon—and British and German times here synchronise with unusual accuracy— he fired three torpedoes from periscope depth at 30-second intervals. The fourth bow tube, which was to have been fired at what the Captain called " a 15,000-ton whale oil factory ship " (probably one of the tankers in the convoy riding high out of the water in ballast) missed fire. Nor did Lemp dive immediately on completing his attack. He stayed at periscope depth to watch the results; and that final incaution probably sealed his fate.

A few seconds *before* the *Esmond* was hit Lieutenant-Commander Smith in the *Aubrietia*, which was then about 4 cables (800 yards) from the starboard wing column, heard the approaching torpedoes on his Asdic set, and at once turned to starboard.[1] At 12.03 he sighted a periscope, and almost simultaneously his Asdic operator, Able Seaman William Samuel Rutledge, obtained a firm contact at about 800 yards. Unluckily the Asdic set then went out of action; but Smith got in a quick attack by eye with a full pattern of 10 charges set to 100 and 225 feet. He realised, however, that it was " a chancy business " and unlikely to produce results. A few minutes later Rutledge reported his instrument in action, and quickly regained contact at 1,700 yards. The U-boat was now steering towards the sinking merchantmen, and at 12.23 Smith attacked it from the port quarter with another full pattern—settings 150 and 385 feet. But the pattern was fired rather late, and he did not at first think it could have been successful. He then closed the sinking *Esmond* to pick up

[1] See Map 4. (opposite).

her survivors. Meanwhile the *Broadway* and the *Bulldog* had both gained firm contact, and were preparing to attack, when a patch of disturbed water attracted everyone's attention. Dozens of pairs of eyes focused on it, and a silence that was almost eerie descended on the three ships. It was broken only by the steady " pings " of the Asdics and the unmistakable " pongs " of a returning submarine echo; but a few guns *did* start to train round in that direction—at first almost with hesitancy.

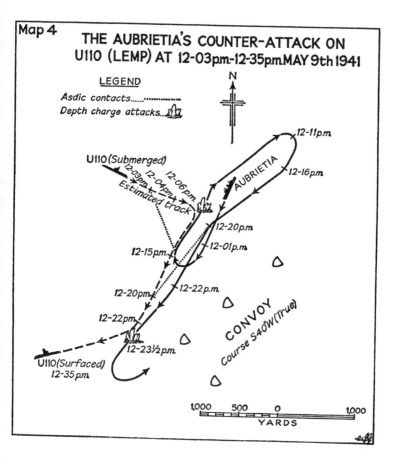

Map 4

THE AUBRIETIA'S COUNTER-ATTACK ON
U110 (LEMP) AT 12-03pm-12-35pm MAY 9th 1941

LEGEND

Asdic contacts....................
Depth charge attacks....

N

12-11p.m.

12-16p.m.

U110 (Submerged)
12-03pm 12-04pm 12-06p.m.
Estimated track

AUBRIETIA

12-20p.m.

12-01p.m.

12-15p.m.

12-20pm.   12-22p.m.

12-22pm.

12-23½p.m.

U110 (Surfaced)
12-35pm.

CONVOY
Course S40°W (True)

1,000   500   0   1,000
YARDS

U.110 broke surface soon after the plumes from the *Aubrietia*'s second pattern had subsided; and then things began to happen extremely fast. In Smith's log the time was recorded as 12.35 p.m., and although the other ships differed slightly we may take that as accurate. It was the sight for which every captain of an anti-submarine vessel prays—and all too rarely sees in a form of warfare in which he is always trying to grapple with an invisible enemy. It is not surprising that first reactions should have been to " see red." After all that evil-looking black shape had just torpedoed two ships, some of whose crews had probably been killed, while others were still floundering in the water. For a few seconds Baker-Cresswell certainly knew that " seeing red " was not entirely a figurative expression, and he was about to give the order to ram when the " redness" cleared and his usual calm returned. Seeing men pour out of the U-boat's conning tower he swung the *Bulldog* off her ramming course. Then, as the Germans clustered around their 4.2-inch gun, he thought that they must mean to fight it out, and gave the order to open fire. The 3-inch HA/LA dual-purpose gun fired the first round, which hit the conning tower; and then every type of weapon joined in. An R.N.V.R. Lieutenant on the bridge picked up a " stripped Lewis gun "— a sort of gangster weapon provided for quick use against low-flying aircraft—and asked if he could open fire. " All right, let them have it," said the Captain, and just as the shattering racket started close to his ear he saw that the Germans were abandoning ship and jumping into the water. All " redness " had now cleared from the escort commander's mind, and he realised that the moment had come when an attempt to capture the enemy might come off. Ordering " Full Speed Astern " on the engines he brought the *Bulldog* to a stop only 100 yards from the U-boat. His next order was " Away Armed Boat's Crew."

Then, to Baker-Cresswell's horror he saw the *Broadway* heading straight for the U-boat, apparently intent on ramming.

He flashed to Taylor to " keep clear," seized the loud-hailer (which could carry a voice over a mile on a calm day) and shouted into it " DO NOT RAM "; but still the *Broadway* came on. Maybe, thought Baker-Cresswell, he is still " seeing red "; but actually Taylor was, by his own account, intending to drop two shallow-set depth charges right under the enemy " with the object of preventing the U-boat diving again, and to force the crew to abandon ship without scuttling or destroying secret material." Moreover the firing of his own 4-inch guns had cracked all his bridge windows so badly that he could not see out of them. It was thus completely unintentional that, in closing the slowly circling U-boat to drop his depth charges, Taylor struck her a glancing blow. The consequences to the destroyer's flimsy plating were serious, for the U-boat's hydroplane (a horizontal fin mounted near the bows, and used for altering trim) tore a big gash in her port bow, holed her badly below the waterline amidships, and knocked off her port propellor. How much the *Broadway*'s effort contributed to the capture of the enemy it is impossible to say; but she certainly damaged herself quite seriously. Baker-Cresswell, who was thinking more of getting his men aboard the U-boat than of the damage sustained by his subordinate, saw the *Broadway* draw clear with relief.

The next step—and the reader should remember that all this happened in a shorter time than it takes to read this account—was to pick up the German survivors, and Baker-Cresswell recalled the *Aubrietia* to carry that out. Captain J. B. McCafferty and the entire crew of 49 officers and men from the *Esmond* had just climbed on board the corvette by the scrambling nets hanging down her port side, when U.110 broke surface on her quarter. A spontaneous cheer at once swept the *Aubrietia*, and no one joined in it more vociferously than the rescued merchant seamen; but the corvette's 4-inch gun's crew were disgusted because the other ships were fouling the range, and they could not therefore open fire. Years later

Lieutenant-Commander Smith wrote, " I suppose I must have felt some excitement, but my impression is that the tension was neither more nor less than in anti-submarine exercises off Tobermory or Londonderry "; which calmness of temperament may account for the remarkable success achieved by his little ship. " Nevertheless " he went on, " we were certainly heartened, after so many months without any tangible contact with the enemy."

Captain McCafferty, for all that he had just passed through the trying ordeal of losing his ship, now watched the gun engagement with the liveliest interest from the *Aubrietia*'s bridge. " My," he remarked at one moment, " the Battle of Trafalgar must have been a snowball fight compared to this! " The *Esmond* must indeed have been a splendidly manned and organised ship. Although she sank quite quickly her whole crew got away in the boats without (in Lieutenant-Commander Smith's words) " even getting their feet wet "; and the very careful victualling of each boat apparently included a case of brandy—a fact which, in the excitement of the moment, no one remembered to mention to the *Aubrietia* until it was too late to salve it! Once on board the corvette all the Merchant Navy survivors settled down to work with their R.N. counterparts. The Chief Officer helped with the navigation, the engineers remade joints and packed glands, while the Boatswain and his men were found busily painting the *Aubrietia*'s bulkheads. Truly the spirit of the British Merchant Navy is incomparable. But Captain McCafferty and his men must have derived considerable satisfaction from watching 34 bedraggled Germans come up the little corvette's side. Few of them had much kick left in them, but one man spat in the face of a Petty Officer, and was promptly pushed back into the sea until he remembered his manners. The prisoners were at once hustled below to a closed compartment whence they could see nothing of what was going on outside the ship. Next Smith told Sub-Lieutenant P. D. Newman, R.N.V.R., who had been in charge of the rescue operation, to make absolutely certain that the few Germans still floating in the water were dead, and on receiving a report that this was so he moved his ship back towards the *Bulldog*. Sub-Lieutenant B. C. Sheen, R.N.V.R. was placed in charge of the prisoners, and after they had stripped off their wet clothes and wrapped themselves in blankets he and a number of willing helpers conducted a preliminary interrogation. Several of the Germans spoke English quite well, but none in the corvette's crew knew any German. None the less they evidently enjoyed their unusual task. Officers' Cook James O'Brien for example " spoke as if I did not like the English in order to encourage the prisoners to talk." Evidently he was not above exploiting his Irish ancestry for the benefit of the country he was now sering. Ecke, the war correspondent, told O'Brien he was " afraid to go to England as it was going to be bombed more heavily than ever before—or to Canada as the U-boats had made the voyage so dangerous." He expected the war to end (presumably in a victory for Germany) " some time after this month "—a statement which, for vagueness, might qualify for inclusion in an astrologer's forecast. O'Brien, himself a cook, was especially interested to learn that the Germans had grape-fruit for breakfast, and had enjoyed fresh food for lunch that very day. When he retailed this information on the mess decks later some of his shipmates said they would volunteer for service in U-boats, as the messing was obviously much better than in corvettes. Able Seaman Joseph Jakeman, who had just been releasing the *Aubrietia*'s depth charges at U.110, and was later " Mentioned in Dispatches " for his share in her capture, also talked with Ecke, who said that their first pattern had done no damage; but the second one had " stopped the engines, put out the lights, and they knew it was the finish for them." This was, by all accounts, very near the truth.

Meanwhile the men detailed for the *Bulldog*'s boarding party, which consisted of six seamen, a stoker, and a telegraphist under Sub-Lieutenant David Edward Balme, R.N., then aged twenty and a half, had armed themselves with rifles, revolvers and hand grenades, which were all kept ready to hand, and manned the five-oared whaler.[1] Balme reported on the bridge, and was told by his Captain " Get on board the U-boat as quickly as you can. I think she is completely abandoned, but there may still be one or two men left on board. Get hold of the documents first, and then anything else useful that you can take away. Never mind if you lose the whaler in getting on board. I will send over another boat." Balme slid quickly down the bridge ladder, and climbed into the whaler, which was then lowered to just above the water and dropped by releasing gear into the heaving Atlantic. The duty was a stern test of seamanship, courage and initiative; but Balme and the whole of his crew welcomed the opportunity wholeheartedly.

What had happened on board U.110 between the *Aubrietia* sighting her periscope at 12.03 and her breaking surface at about 12.35? It is difficult to piece together a coherent

---

[1] The names of the men who went across in the *Bulldog*'s whaler and seized U.110 should be recorded in full. They were as follows:—

> Allen Osborne Long, Telegraphist
> Sidney George Pearce, Able Seaman
> Cyril Arthur George Dolley, Able Seaman
> Richard Roe, Able Seaman
> Claude Arthur Wileman, Able Seaman
> Arnold Hargreaves, Able Seaman
> John Trotter, Able Seaman
> Cyril George Lee, Stoker 1st Class

Except for Long, who was a short-service rating, they were long-service men; all came from the Portsmouth manning depot. Long was awarded the Distinguished Service Medal " for obtaining valuable information from U.110." All the others were " Mentioned in Dispatches " for " good work in salving documents under conditions of danger and difficulty."

story from the fragmentary recollections of those of her crew who escaped—not least because neither Lemp nor Wehrhofer survived. The Captain was seen swimming in the water, and apparently asked Loewe and Eichelborn about the junior officer's fate—for he remembered that Wehrhofer had only recently returned to duty after recovering from a serious illness. Evidently Lemp's care for his crew never failed him. Loewe, the First Lieutenant, Eichelborn the Engineer, and Ecke the war correspondent (who had been given temporary naval rank), were the senior survivors, and from what they and certain of the ratings later told their interrogators it is fairly clear that, shortly before the *Aubrietia* fired her first pattern at 12.06 Lemp pulled down the periscope and went deep. He then altered course about 90° to starboard, and the first depth charges did no damage; but they knew that the attacker was still in Asdic contact. They then heard the *Aubrietia* pass overhead, and her second pattern exploded, with deadly effect, a short while later. The Germans declared that 18 charges were heard, but we know that only 10 were fired. According to survivors the interior of the boat " was wrecked "—a statement which does not at all tally with the conditions found by the *Bulldog*'s boarding party; the hydroplanes, rudder, electric motors and compasses were all put out of action; oil entered the hull from a damaged fuel tank, gas was given off from a damaged battery, she took up a trim by the stern, and the crew rushed towards the bows in panic. Loewe, who seems to have kept his head, is alleged to have suggested to Ecke, who only that morning had been taking dozens of pictures of the meeting with U.201, that he should photograph the faces of the panic-struck crew. The U-boat is supposed to have gone down to 95 metres (about 310 feet); but that seems improbable. Lemp then ordered the ballast tanks to be blown; but the control lever had been smashed, and no one could explain how she came to the surface. Indeed the crew only realised that she had done so when they felt a gentle rocking motion. The conning tower hatch was then opened, and Lemp gave the order to abandon ship. He himself hustled them over the side, but some were killed by our ships' gunfire. The rest of their story has already been told.

CHAPTER VIII

Capture and Search

As soon as Balme's whaler had been dropped into the water he pointed her towards the U-boat, his men got out their oars, and they pulled lustily across the short intervening space of water. The sea was, for the Atlantic, comparatively calm; but that did not mean that it was an easy matter to handle a small and heavily laden boat bound on such a venture.

Although quite large waves were breaking over the U-boat's hull, Balme skilfully took the whaler alongside her forward of the conning tower. His bowman at once jumped aboard with the rope painter and held the boat, while he himself, quickly followed by the rest of the boarding party, scrambled on to the deck. Not for the first time had the training the Royal Navy gives to all junior officers in handling boats under oars and sail, as well as under power, proved its value. As he walked aft Balme drew his revolver, feeling very conscious of the fact that his capacity to use the weapon was, to say the least, doubtful. Years later he wrote " Had anyone appeared I do not suppose I would have hit him, but the revolver gave me a sense of security for I *did* expect someone to come out of the conning tower." He next climbed up on to the conning tower, found the hatch open, and looked down into the inside of the U-boat. All seemed very quiet below, but it was hard to believe that some of her crew were not still there, trying to scuttle their helpless ship. " To climb down the conning tower of a submarine when one has hardly ever been aboard one before," wrote Balme, " is difficult enough with both hands free, and to do so with a loaded revolver in one hand seemed likely to prove suicidal. So I put the revolver back into its holster. This to me was the worst moment of the whole affair, since while I was climbing down I was presenting a perfect target to anyone below." He was soon followed by the rest of the boarding party, and Baker-Cresswell, who was watching anxiously from the *Bulldog*'s bridge now knew that the prize was almost certainly secured.

When Balme reached the bottom of the conning tower ladder he found no sign of life. All the lights were still burning, and " everything was lying around just as if one had arrived at someone's house after breakfast, before they had time to make the beds. Coats were flung around, and bunks half made. There was complete silence in the U-boat except for the continual thud-thud of our own ships' depth charges. This was a most unpleasant sound," he wrote later, " especially when the detonations came closer—for it made one expect the U-boat to be blown up at any moment. However, we wasted no time and started immediately looking at the gear and documents lying around. The Telegraphist in the boarding party (whose name was Allen Osborne Long) immediately went to the wireless office, noted all the setting on the U-boat's wireless sets, and dismantled a lot of equipment. Meanwhile I had a look at some of the charts, and at once noticed the heavy dark lines indicating all the searched channels leading into the German U-boat bases. Two or three of the seamen now helped me pass all the charts up through the conning tower and into the whaler, and they were soon followed by all the books. One had no time to distinguish between those of greater or less importance, so we passed out the whole lot. Various pieces of movable equipment which were obviously of technical interest were also sent up, and we also found about half a dozen sextants of superb quality—far superior to those supplied to us by the Admiralty. Of course I know nothing about the use that was later made of what we seized, but from my own personal point of view the greatest find was about ten pairs of Super Zeiss binoculars. One of them, I am afraid, was not handed in; and I still use it nearly every week-end when I am out sailing. They are the finest I have ever used, and the same standard applied to everything else we found in the U-boat. For instance those were the days when England was short of everything, and we all lacked clothing which was really suitable for work on the Atlantic convoy route; but in the U-boat we found quantities of splendid leather clothing—similar to what we later, and enviously, saw American sailors wearing. While inside the U-boat we lost all sense of time, but I believe the whaler made several trips backwards and forwards loaded down with documents and equipment. In due course our Engineer Officer came over to see if he could get machinery started, but he had no success."

While Balme and his men were exploring the inside of the U-boat every pair of eyes on the upper decks of the *Bulldog*, *Broadway* and *Aubrietia* was anxiously watching her. Would she sink with the British sailors trapped inside her? What were they finding? Could they tow the prize in? How badly damaged was she? Such and a dozen other similar questions were passing through everyone's minds. Outside the Engine Room hatch of the *Bulldog* a furious argument was in progress. The First Lieutenant, John Aitken, had just restrained the young doctor from jumping overboard to help rescue the Germans bobbing about in the water, while Lieutenant-Commander G. E. Dodds, the R.N.R. Engineer Officer was telling him not to be a silly unmentionable, and threatening a very unpleasant fate for any Germans on whom he himself might lay his hands. The Captain, overhearing this, remembered an argument between the same two in the wardroom a short while earlier, when the doctor had declared that he would never help to rescue German U-boat sailors, but Dodds had said, " I don't agree at all. After all they are only doing their duty like you or me."

But the Captain had little time now to consider the ethics of such arguments; for he was very conscious not only that Balme and his crew, marooned on board the U-boat, might be in grave danger, but that his three ships were presenting a perfect target to any other enemy which might be about. The visibility was now closing down rapidly, and the convoy had disappeared over the misty southern horizon; but the distant thud of depth charge explosions made it clear that another attack was in progress. Baker-Cresswell's next order was to the *Broadway* to send her American-type motor-boat, a larger and more seaworthy craft than the British whalers, over to the U-boat; and Taylor got her away very promptly. Secondly the group commander organised an anti-submarine patrol around the prize. It was now nearly 2.30 p.m., and the precautions against U-boat attack were not taken a moment too early; for hardly had the *Bulldog* started to patrol when her Asdic produced echoes which she identified as submarine, and which were quickly confirmed by both the *Aubrietia* and *Broadway*. During the next hour (2.35–3.35 p.m.) the three ships were almost continuously in contact with what they were convinced was another U-boat. The *Aubrietia* made two attacks, and the *Broadway* three, while the *Bulldog* helped the others to hold the contact, and kept an anxious eye all the time on the prize. By 3.40, however, the contact had faded out without yielding any evidence to show that the attacks had inflicted damage. We will return later to the question of whether these contacts were on a genuine submarine.

With Balme and his crew down below on board U.110, and the three ships watchfully patrolling around her, we must temporarily take leave of them and return to the convoy, which we left at the time of Lemp's noon attack. The rescue of the *Esmond*'s entire crew by the *Aubrietia* has already been described; but the *Bengore Head*'s men were little less fortunate. Although the ship was hit right amidships, and broke in two immediately " the funnel falling forward on to the bridge and the two masts crossing," only one of the forty-five in her crew was killed. All the rest were picked up either by the trawler *St. Apollo* or by the Norwegian ship *Borgfred*, which had joined the convoy from Iceland on the evening of 7th.[1] The Chief Officer of the *Bengore Head* declared with some indignation that, had the *Empire Caribou* (No. 81) not been astern of station at the time, it would have been she that was hit.[2] But in fact that ship was not to survive many hours longer; and if they ever heard of her fate[3], the *Bengore Head*'s men would doubtless have forgiven the earlier lapse.

The mess-boy in the *Borgfred* was a West Indian lad of Portuguese descent from Trinidad called Alfred Mendes, then aged twenty. On the outbreak of war he was at college in the United States; but in 1940 he decided that it was his duty to take an active part in the war, and signed on for the Merchant Navy. In 1958 he was working as an oil driller in Tripoli, and from his camp in the desert he wrote to tell the author of this book how vividly some of the incidents which took place during the passage of convoy OB.318 had remained in his memory. His ship, which had taken station at the rear of the starboard wing column, had been told to act as rescue ship in the event of U-boat attack, and as soon as the *Esmond* and *Bengore Head* were torpedoed she therefore moved across to pick up survivors. " One of them," wrote Mr. Mendes, " was a young mess-boy from the *Bengore Head*, and his rescue will always be remembered by me as a classic example of Norwegian seamanship. We had already taken on board all the survivors we could see, and were moving ahead again, when someone spotted this boy in the water some way off on our port quarter. Before the *Borgfred* had lost way again our Bosun, a big Norwegian whalefisher called Per Strøm, and one or two A.B.s had lowered the small lifeboat, and were on their way to pick him up; but in spite of all we could do for him the boy died from exposure. His subsequent burial at sea was

[1] See p. 85.   [2] See Map 3 (p. 107).   [3] See p. 146.

witnessed by three Captains—our own and the two we had rescued. Where the surfacing of the U-boat fitted into this hectic sequence of events I cannot recollect; but I remember seeing it on the surface only a short distance away on our starboard quarter. Of course I was very surprised to learn not only that she was captured, but that there were survivors from her; for it seemed to me that the escort vessels were expending all their ammunition on the luckless U-boat. Moreover had her fate been left in the hands of our First Mate, Mr. Sabo, she *would* have been blown to smithereens! He was in charge of our 4-inch gun, and on seeing the submarine break surface he immediately trained it on to the target, and shouted the order to open fire. To this day I can remember his fearful rage and bitter disappointment when his order produced no answering ' bang '; and the way in which the offending ' dud ' shell was cast overboard certainly reflected his mood. Nor did he get a second chance; for the water around the U-boat was soon cluttered with escort ships. After the convoy dispersed the old *Borgfred*, a coal burner built in 1921, made her way to Sydney, Nova Scotia, as fast as her tired boilers could push her, the 25 in our crew making room for the 49 extra souls we had on board."

When Baker-Cresswell took the *Bulldog* off the screen to start the hunt for U.110 a few minutes after noon, Lieutenant-Commander Roper of the *Amazon* took charge of the escort. He stationed his own ship and the *Hollyhock* ahead of the convoy, and ordered the *Nigella* to move across to cover the starboard beam. The trawler *Daneman* was already on the port beam, but the *St. Apollo* was still picking up the *Bengore Head*'s survivors, while the third trawler, the *Angle*, which had been with the convoy since it set out from Britain, had just been detached to Iceland because she was running short of fuel.[1] Roper thus had only four ships with him—a very tenuous

[1] See p. 59.

screen for a large convoy; and a signal from Lieutenant T. W. Coyne, R.N.R., of the *Nigella* reporting that his Asdic set was out of action made matters even worse; for Roper realised that the whole starboard side of the convoy was thus virtually unprotected. Without a moment's hesitation he increased speed, swung round his *Amazon* and swept down the exposed flank.

Meanwhile Commodore Mackenzie had made another

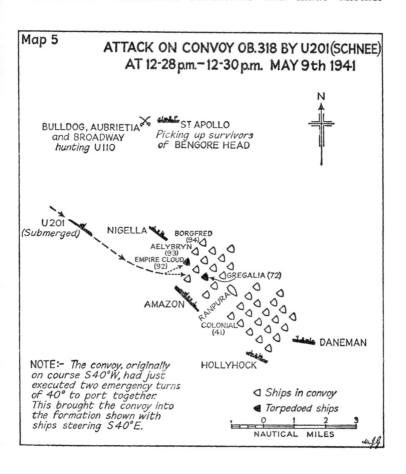

Map 5

ATTACK ON CONVOY OB.318 BY U201(SCHNEE) AT 12-28p.m.–12-30p.m. MAY 9th 1941

N

BULLDOG, AUBRIETIA and BROADWAY hunting U110

ST APOLLO
Picking up survivors of BENGORE HEAD

U201 (Submerged)

NIGELLA

BORGFRED (94)
AELYBRYN (93)
EMPIRE CLOUD (92)

GREGALIA (72)

AMAZON

RANPURA

COLONIAL (41)

DANEMAN

HOLLYHOCK

NOTE:– *The convoy, originally on course S40°W, had just executed two emergency turns of 40° to port together. This brought the convoy into the formation shown with ships steering S40°E.*

◁ Ships in convoy
◀ Torpedoed ships

0   1   2   3
NAUTICAL MILES

emergency turn to port, bringing the convoy on to course South 40° East (true); and at about the same moment the A.M.C. *Ranpura* reported sighting a periscope $1\frac{1}{2}$ miles to the west of her. It was a sharp-eyed Able Seaman named Cyril Edward Madden who first saw it, and he was later " mentioned in dispatches " for his alertness. A few minutes after the *Ranpura*, the *Chaucer* (No. 82) also reported sighting the periscope; but these glimpses of a new enemy did not save the convoy from further attack. At 12.28 p.m. the *Empire Cloud* (No. 92) and the *Gregalia* (No. 72), which had both been placed virtually at the rear of the convoy by the two recently executed emergency turns, were torpedoed almost simultaneously on their starboard sides. The *Amazon* was only about 6 cables (1,200 yards) from the *Empire Cloud* when she was struck, and Roper promptly dropped a depth charge and altered towards the convoy. At 12.29 his Asdic produced a contact only 500 yards ahead which he immediately classified as " submarine." There is no doubt that this was Schnee's U.201, which had followed Lemp's U.110 after precisely half an hour's interval—as the two U-boat commanders had agreed.

Schnee's report states that he started to move in to attack just before 11 a.m., but was forced to dive by " two destroyers," and dared not risk surfacing again. He therefore remained submerged, and used his periscope only very occasionally. He passed between two of the escorts on the screen ahead of the convoy (presumably the *Amazon* and *Hollyhock*), and dived under what he described as an " auxiliary vessel " at the head of Column 8.[1]

At 12.26 he fired two torpedoes from his bow tubes at a " 12,000-ton transport " (actually the *Empire Cloud* of 5,968 tons), and claimed that both hit. Two minutes later he fired a stern torpedo tube at a " 6,000-ton freighter ", and heard

[1] Schnee actually said " the 2nd column from the left," presumably as viewed from ahead of the convoy, *i.e.*, Column 8 on the British diagram. See Map 5 (p. 123).

another explosion. This must have been the hit on the *Gregalia*. A " zig-zag by the convoy "—probably the emergency turn ordered by the Commodore—then forced him to dive, and " almost at once a well-placed pattern of depth charges " made him go deeper. This marked the beginning of a prolonged counter-attack by the *Amazon*, *Nigella* and *St. Apollo*.

With two merchantmen apparently sinking, a U-boat very close to the convoy, one of his four ships without Asdic, and his own *Amazon* very short of depth charges, Roper had to face a difficult situation. The first and plainest need was to keep the U-boat down, and he himself therefore made an immediate " pounce " attack. Five depth charges were dropped (settings 150–385 feet), after which he lost contact, but soon regained it at 1,000 yards range. He now had only seven depth charges left, and for his second attack at 12.34 did not dare expend more than three of them. After the plumes had subsided he once more regained firm contact, but the *Amazon* could now do little more than direct the attacks of other ships. Lieutenant Davies of the *Hollyhock* had meanwhile been told to take charge of the convoy, and Lieutenant Coyne's *Nigella* was coming across to join in the hunt.

At 12.45 Roper released a single depth charge on his contact, and ordered Coyne to add a full pattern by eye. This was unlikely to produce results, but it was the best that could be done. Then, seeing the *Empire Cloud*'s and *Gregalia*'s boats pulling their way and " likely to foul the course " he told Coyne to pick up the survivors. Captain C. Brown of the *Empire Cloud* described later how, after his ship was struck he " looked around " and found that the engine room and stokehold were flooded, the starboard boats smashed, and water was pouring into No. 4 hold. The port boats were lowered, and in them and on some rafts all except five of his crew of 50 got away safely. The ship meanwhile remained afloat, and on an even keel; but was wholly without motive power. The hole in her starboard side was so large that the men on the *Amazon*'s bridge could see that her main engines had been blown right across the ship and out of the port side. After the *Nigella* had rescued the men from the *Empire Cloud*'s boats Roper signalled for volunteers to reboard the ship, since prospects of salvaging her appeared good. We will return to the subsequent adventures of the damaged ship shortly.

While the *Nigella* was picking up the *Empire Cloud*'s men, the *Aelybryn* (No. 93) had left her position in the convoy and closed the *Gregalia*'s boats, from which she and another merchantman rescued the entire crew of 52; and Lieutenant Marchington's *St. Apollo* was steering to join the *Amazon* in the hunt for the assailant. It was the little trawler who next reported a contact, quite close to the *Empire Cloud*; and she quickly made two attacks, each with six depth charges. A few minutes later, just after 1 p.m., the *Amazon* dropped her last three. Oil and air bubbles came to the surface; but Roper was too old a hand at the game to think such portents proved that he had damaged the enemy. He considered it more likely that the U-boat was merely altering her trim. Next the *Nigella* dropped a pattern on top of the *Amazon*'s, after which the contact faded. Roper now ordered a sweep to the north, and the *Amazon*, *Nigella* and *St. Apollo* were steaming slowly in that direction when, just after 3 p.m. the trawler regained contact. Lieutenant Marchington, evidently no respecter of persons, boldly " signalled to the *Amazon* to keep clear," and attacked. The detonation of his pattern was followed by " a further marked, rather dull explosion and an upheaval of blackish coloured water." His look-outs hopefully, but too optimistically, shouted " submarine surfacing "; but the waters subsided without revealing a black shape, and all that Marchington could do was to mark the position with an oil drum. Next the *Nigella* attacked with the *St. Apollo* directing her, after which Roper's Asdic operator reported hearing 5 or 6 faint under-water explosions; but they may have come from the depth charges which the *Bulldog* and her consorts were dropping around U.110 a few miles away to the north.[1] Between 4 and 4.30 p.m. Marchington made two more attacks. There was now an area of about a square mile covered with oil. As the *Esmond, Bengore Head, Empire Cloud* and *Gregalia* were all coal-burning ships, they could not have been the origin of it; the captured U.110 was 3 or 4 miles away, and although the oil might have come from her, or from the *Broadway*'s damaged fuel tanks, it did seem likely that this third assailant (which we now know to have been U.201) had suffered damage. When, however, 6 p.m. came and none of the ships had regained contact, Roper reported the situation by voice radio to Baker-Cresswell, who was now out of sight to the north. The senior officer decided that the *Nigella* and *St. Apollo* should stay on patrol near the position of the last contact, while Roper went to look for the *Empire Cloud*, which had meanwhile drifted out of sight to the east. He found her still afloat, though down by the stern, and the prospects of salvage still appeared good. By 6.30 p.m. he had rejoined the *Nigella* and *St. Apollo*, and transferred some of the *Empire Cloud*'s crew from them to his own *Amazon*. Half an hour later the *Aubrietia* hove in sight, and from her Roper collected a further 27 Merchant Navy survivors, and all the German prisoners. Two of the latter had died on board Smith's corvette, leaving 32 to be transferred to the *Amazon*. They had evidently recovered by this time from the shock of the disaster to their own ship, and the loss of so many of their comrades; for Roper's chief recollection is that their behaviour was so arrogant that his First Lieutenant had difficulty in restraining some of his own ship's company from dealing with them drastically. The simultaneous presence in a small destroyer of a large body of prisoners, who had been captured in such unusual circumstances, and a considerable number of Merchant Navy survivors provided some very tricky problems. Plainly the need for security regarding the manner of the capture of

[1] See p. 120.

the Germans was paramount, and Roper took steps to emphasise to the Merchant Navy men that on no account must they reveal what they might have seen or heard. Apart from the compartment in which the Germans were confined, the British survivors were allowed the free run of the entire *Amazon*, whose officers gave up their own cabins and did their utmost to make them comfortable. Great therefore was Roper's astonishment to learn later that some of the *Empire Cloud*'s and *Bengore Head*'s men had complained, on their return to England, that he had " arrested " them, and that they had been " treated as prisoners " while on board his ship. The complaints reached the Admiralty, who asked Admiral Noble to investigate the matter. A mass of statements was collected, and from them it became obvious that the complaints were utterly without foundation. It was all very strange and unusual; for the Merchant Navy men more commonly expressed their heartfelt appreciation for all that their rescuers did for them. Indeed, as Roper pointed out, he had actually received a letter from the Ulster Steamship Company, owners of the *Bengore Head*, thanking him for his care for the survivors from their ship; and the Master of the *Empire Cloud* had actually slept in his own First Lieutenant's cabin while on board. The probability is that the emphasis placed on security was genuinely misunderstood by a few of the survivors, and that one or two disgruntled " sea lawyers " then fabricated the rest of the story. But the quick action taken by the Admiralty and Admiral Noble to investigate the matter at least showed how deeply the Royal Navy cared for its reputation for wholehearted hospitality towards our merchant seamen in distress.

The transfer of prisoners and survivors from the *Aubrietia* to the *Amazon* had to be made in boats which had belonged to the torpedoed merchantmen; for the wind and sea were now rising rapidly, and it was too rough to use warships' boats. By 9 p.m. the exchange was completed. Roper then sent the *Aubrietia* and *Nigella* to the rendezvous with the next east-bound convoy (HX.124), told the *St. Apollo* to look after the helpless *Empire Cloud*, round which he himself made a final sweep; and then, just before midnight, he turned the *Amazon*'s head towards Reykjavik. When he was fifty miles clear he signalled to the Flag Officer in Charge, Iceland, giving the damaged merchantman's position, and asking for a tug to be sent. That same evening, when all was quiet, Smith of the *Aubrietia* was discussing the day's events with his Coxswain, and said he thought they had attacked three different U-boats. He received the confident and cheering reply, " Sir, we sank three; but we attacked five! "

So ended the long hunt for Schnee's U.201. On the British side there appeared to be good grounds for believing that she had been seriously damaged, if not sunk. Captain D. K. Bain, who was the 3rd Escort Group's administrative authority at Greenock, was confident that the target attacked by the *Amazon*, *Nigella* and *St. Apollo* had been a U-boat, and considered that, although firm evidence was lacking, " the enemy was probably damaged." Admiral Noble was rather more optimistic, and in forwarding the report stated it as his opinion that the enemy " was obviously damaged, and it is considered probable that contact was lost because the U-boat sank outside Asdic range. He sent his congratulations to the three ships concerned.

We are now able to gain a clear view of what actually happened to U.201 from Schnee's own report. He stated that the counter-attack lasted from 12.30 to 5.05 p.m., during which time he counted 99 depth charges. He took evasive action each time he heard his adversaries moving into attack, but when he discovered that all the charges were exploding above him he varied his depth only slightly. He described our ships as attacking alternately from port and starboard, and laying accurate patterns of four or five depth charges. Throughout the hunt he " heard the well-known ' pings ' of our Asdics "— for which he coined the pleasantly onomatopoeic word

" Ziepsenden " (which does not appear in the author's German dictionary)—and also noises " like gravel being hurled against his hull "; and he considered that we were dropping small explosive charges to produce echoes from the U-boat. It is difficult to account for the " gravel," and we certainly were not using small charges in the manner suggested. By 7 p.m. he was still hearing Asdic " pings," but no propeller noises; so he came quietly up to periscope depth, only to sight two anti-submarine vessels. They, however, did not see his periscope, and he was able to creep away in safety " at quietest speed." We cannot be quite sure which of the 3rd Escort Group Schnee sighted when he took his cautious look around; but the balance of probability seems to lie with the *Amazon* and *Aubrietia* which, as we have seen, were stopped and engaged in the transfer of the prisoners and Merchant Navy survivors at exactly that time. It is, however, possible that the U-boat commander glimpsed the *Bulldog* and *Broadway*, and failed to notice that the former had an object in tow. Whichever is correct it was lucky for the British ships that Schnee was thinking only of making his getaway, and was anxious not to invite further attacks.

At 9.15 Schnee came to the surface, withdrew to the southeast and licked his wounds. His tale of damage was a long one, and included a leaky external fuel tank—which he considered had given away his presence during the hunt—besides damage to battery casings and air bottles. He had many gauges and instruments broken, and his steering gear and gyro compass had failed temporarily during the attacks, but had been repaired. Most of the damage was made good during the next few days, and on 10th he reported to Lorient that he would be ready to resume operations in two days' time. Dönitz ordered him only to return to port if he was unable to stop the oil leak, and as he had seven torpedoes left he finally decided to stay on patrol in the area assigned to him. One must certainly class Schnee among the more successful and resolute U-boat commanders. Post-war analysis made in Germany credits him with sinking a total of 24 ships (122,987 tons), and places him 22nd in the order of achievements.[1] It is indeed interesting to find that three out of the four U-boat commanders who attacked OB.318 (Kuppisch, Lemp and Schnee) figure in the German list which names the twenty-four most successful exponents of that type of warfare.

There remains the tantalising problem of identifying the target so confidently attacked by the *Bulldog*, *Aubrietia* and *Broadway* near to the position in which U.110 had been captured between 2.35 and 3.36 p.m., and again, though less confidently, between 4.37 and 5.06. All three ships were at the time convinced that another U-boat was present, and that their contacts were genuine; and in analysing the attacks on OB.318 on 9th May the Admiralty accepted their view. At first sight the most likely candidate for the role of additional target is U.556; but a glance at her reports proves that on the afternoon of 9th she was still pursuing the convoy, and her log shows that she underwent no attacks on that day. A very careful check on the movements of all other U-boats which were in the North Atlantic at the time makes it certain that, except for U.94 on 7th May, none of them ever became involved with the escorts of OB.318; and the conclusion that, on the afternoon of 9th, only U.110 and U.201 were on the scene thus becomes inescapable. There is a possibility, though not a very likely one, that the contact attacked by the *Bulldog*'s group was wreckage from a recently sunk merchantman; but three experienced Asdic operators in three different ships would surely not have been simultaneously misled on such a matter. To this writer the balance of probability seems to lie with the suggestion that *both* groups of ships (*Bulldog*, *Broadway*, *Aubrietia* near to the captured U.110 and *Amazon*, *Nigella* and *St. Apollo* near to the damaged *Empire Cloud*) were involved with Schnee's U.201. Throughout

[1] See *Marine Rundschau*, for October 1957.

the afternoon the distance between the two groups was only
3 or 4 miles, and a submerged U-boat of her class could travel
that distance in well under an hour. Schnee said in his report
that the counter-attacks lasted from 12.30 to 5.05 p.m.,
and that he counted 99 depth charges; but we know that the
Amazon, Nigella and *St. Apollo* between them only fired or
released 64 to which the *Bulldog, Broadway* and *Aubrietia* added
another 30 after U.110 had been blown to the surface at 12.35
p.m. Thus the total of depth charges released by the two
groups of British ships tallies surprisingly accurately with
the number counted by Schnee. On the other hand it is true
that ships of both groups, though separated by several miles,
attacked at too closely spaced intervals for us to state with
assurance that U.201 was the target in all of them. Thus the
problem cannot be conclusively solved. All that can be said
with reasonable certainty is, firstly, that the *Amazon*'s group
definitely attacked U.201; secondly that the *Bulldog*'s group
could have done so; and lastly that if the latter's target was
not that U-boat they were attacking false echoes of some
kind or other.

For two days after the departure of all her consorts on the
evening of the 9th the *St. Apollo* faithfully stood by the *Empire
Cloud*. As the expected tug had not turned up, and the weather
was then deteriorating still further, Marchington decided to
try and tow in the helpless merchantman himself. He got a
party of his men on board, veered the *Empire Cloud*'s cable,
and managed to get the end of it on board his own ship. He
then towed her towards Iceland for another two days, after
which he met the corvette *Anemone* and the rescue tug *Thames*,
which had sailed from Reykjavik on the evening of 13th.
Marchington then transferred his tow to the tug, and escorted
her and the *Empire Cloud* all the way to Greenock, where they
arrived safely on 20th May. The *St. Apollo* had by that time
been at sea for over a fortnight, and as she still had a score of
the *Bengore Head*'s survivors on board, very little by way of

fuel or food remained in the trawler; but her whole exploit had been a fine feat of seamanship. Six months later, to be precise on 22nd November, 1941, the *St. Apollo* herself was sunk in collision while escorting a convoy whose Commodore was, by a remarkable coincidence, sailing in the repaired *Empire Cloud*. It was then the turn of Marchington and his men to take the part of survivors in the presence of the ship which they had so recently helped to salvage.

The attacks on the convoy on 9th May made a deep impression on the young clergyman travelling in the *Burma*, who, of course, knew nothing about the capture of U.110 which had followed so quickly on Lemp's noonday attack, but had only seen the *Esmond* and *Bengore Head*, and then the *Empire Cloud* and *Gregalia*, hit by torpedoes; and he believed them all to have been sunk. He headed the entry in his " log " " Black Day " and described the events he had witnessed in the following words:—

" The appalling happenings of to-day place even those of Wednesday in the background. We are in mid-ocean; the weather is still a bit dismal with a cold north-west wind and rather a choppy sea. The first ' bang ' came at 2 p.m. (noon G.M.T.) when the ship on our starboard bow was hit amidships by a torpedo. She crumpled up, her back was broken, but we could see one boat getting away from her. We had not reached our ' action stations ' before a second torpedo sent up another big tramp steamer in a cloud of smoke and steam. This vessel was the first to sink, and it was terrible to see her going down with her stern high in the air. Then an ominous quarter of an hour passed before a second attack came. This time the victims (two big vessels) were on our port side, only 500 yards away. We felt that we ourselves might be struck at any moment, and have to take to the boats in the heaving waters of the mid-Atlantic; but if we were afraid no one showed it. The spirit of the passengers, women and children, and of the crew, was wonderful. Destroyers dropped depth charges, but four more of the convoy went down before our eyes—making six in all lost so far. It was sickening and dreadful, and I will write no more about it . . . the rest of the day and the following night passed in great tension."

We must now return to the prize, and see how Balme and his men had meanwhile fared. After searching the control room and officers' quarters, and removing from them every book, document or piece of movable equipment they could find, they ransacked the rest of the submarine equally thoroughly. Among the trophies recovered were diaries kept both by Lemp and Eichelborn, which told us a good deal not only about U.110's movements but about Lemp's previous command, U.30. Balme later described the prize as " a fine new ship spotlessly clean throughout," and equipped with a " magnificent galley." All our men seem to have been greatly impressed with the quality of the U-boat sailors' food. They found several cameras, and with one of them the enterprising Sub-Lieutenant took cinematograph pictures of the inside of the prize.

Soon after the boarding party first disappeared down the conning tower hatch Baker-Cresswell received a signal saying that there was no one onboard. Through his binoculars he next saw things being passed up on deck and handed down into the *Broadway*'s motor boat. Balme's second message made it plain that what they were finding might be of immense value, and his Captain now became anxious lest the motor boat should be swamped in the steadily rising sea. However the first load soon came safely across to the *Bulldog*, and as the captured material was passed inboard the report came that U.110 had a slight list, but appeared to be in no danger of sinking. Baker-Cresswell therefore sent his Engineer Officer, Lieutenant-Commander G. E. Dodds, R.N.R., his Torpedo

Gunner, Mr. W. J. Gray, and two Engine Room Artificers back in the boat to see if they could increase the submarine's buoyancy. With them he sent across a White Ensign, with an order to Balme to hoist it above the German colours, but as no specimen of the flag with the crooked cross could be found in the submarine he was deprived of the pleasure of seeing his prize adorned in the traditional manner with " the King's colours flying and the enemy's hanging."

When Dodds and his assistants, none of whom had been trained in submarine machinery nor could read German well enough to translate tallies and instructions in that language, got onboard they went straight to the machinery spaces to see if they could discover how things worked. As Dodds went aft he had to pass through a watertight door, which swung to and trapped him. Balme happened to see the Engineer Officer's predicament, and wrote later that he " would never forget the sight of the Chief stuck in the watertight door. It must have been very painful to him, but it was extremely funny to see the look on his face, with the depth charges exploding all around and he firmly stuck in the doorway." The humour of the situation might not have been apparent to anyone except a Sub-Lieutenant aged twenty. Dodds's own recollection is that during the few minutes (or were they only seconds?) that passed before he could get the door open again he really knew what fear was. He and his assistants then tried to make out which of the innumerable valves and levers controlled what; but it was really a forlorn hope. They dared not turn valves or pull levers indiscriminately, because it might produce the opposite to the desired result; and all the time they could not get rid of the thought that there were probably scuttling charges somewhere in the boat, and that a false movement might set them off.

Dodds found the pressure hull of the U-boat dry, but in the after compartments it had been buckled and water was seeping in from a leak somewhere. As she rolled the outer plates creaked ominously, and he could hear a slight bubbling noise, probably caused by air escaping from the high pressure bottles, or from the inside of the boat into the sea; but he could not trace its source, nor guess how to stop it. While still searching the machinery compartments our ships began to drop depth charges in the vicinity, and Dodds found the pressure waves which hit the hull " as if with a huge hammer," " rather distracting "; but he persisted with his inspection until he was convinced that he could do nothing to improve the U-boat's seaworthiness. Then he joined up with Balme's party in collecting charts and books and passing them into the waiting motor boat, where willing hands took them. Not one of the items recovered was lost or damaged.

Balme and Dodds now signalled to the *Bulldog* by lamp and semaphore reporting the condition of the prize, and Baker-Cresswell racked his brains to find the best way of getting her into port. In none of the three ships present was there a single officer or man with submarine experience. Should he put one or two Germans back on board and try and force them to work their ship? No sooner had the thought passed through his mind than he discarded it as hopeless; for he knew that they would never carry out such orders, except perhaps under a degree of duress which he could not dream of applying. At last came a report from Balme that he had sent across every piece of movable equipment he could find, and Baker-Cresswell passed the word to " Batten down and prepare to be taken in tow." It was now 4 p.m., about three hours after the boarding party had first been sent across.

But for a destroyer to take a submarine in tow, especially in a rising sea, is not as easy as it sounds; since a submarine's deck is extremely narrow, and in the bows there is only room for one or two men to stand in order to take the heavy wire and secure it to her bollards. Thus the *Bulldog*'s stern had to be manœuvred as close as possible to her prize, whose sharp bow could do serious damage to a destroyer's thin plating—as the *Broadway*'s very recent experience had shown only too convincingly. Dodds and one or two men worked their way forward, and finally succeeded in passing the end of the *Bulldog*'s 3½-inch wire through the U-boat's towing eye, and successfully securing it. As there was now no point in leaving anyone onboard the U-boat, Baker-Cresswell recalled the last of his men in the *Broadway*'s boat, which he then hoisted into his own ship; but his troubles were by no means yet ended.

U.110's rudder was jammed with port wheel on, and no sooner had the *Bulldog* gone gently ahead to take the strain on the tow than she began to sheer off to port. To get her to ride easily Baker-Cresswell had to use a long tow, and to prevent the wire being parted by a sudden surge it was essential to give it as much " spring " as possible. He therefore shackled his kedge anchor to the towing wire, and paid them out together; but a wave hit the anchor, spun it several times round the towing wire and jammed the two together. This prevented the tow being lengthened to the desired degree; but none the less the prize rode reasonably comfortably on the port quarter of the towing ship. Just when everything seemed set as well as could be expected, a look-out reported " Periscope on the starboard bow." The *Bulldog* had no contact on her own Asdic; but Baker-Cresswell could not afford to risk getting a torpedo into his ship while she was virtually a sitting duck. He therefore slipped the tow, and carried out a search. The *Broadway* and *Aubrietia* both reported Asdic contacts, and the latter dropped a single depth charge. But the contacts could not be verified, and after searching carefully around the prize they were assumed to have been false. It is tempting to suggest that the periscope belonged to Schnee's U.201, which was certainly lurking in the depths not very far away at the time; but according to his log it was 7 p.m. when he cautiously raised it, and that does not correspond with the time of the contacts reported by the *Broadway* and *Aubrietia*. Moreover if Schnee really did glimpse the *Bulldog* and her consorts it is hard to believe that he could have failed to see that the British destroyer had some object in tow.

Baker-Cresswell waited for half an hour, and at 5 p.m. decided to pick up the tow; but his wire was, of course, now hanging uselessly from U.110's bow, and he first had to recover it. Having successfully accomplished that first step he then had to repeat the anxious manœuvre of placing his own stern as close as possible to the U-boat's bow. This time they just touched, and the *Bulldog* received a slight dent in her plating. Months later, when the ship was refitting on the Clyde, and dockyard workmen wished to repair the damaged plate the Captain flatly refused to have it touched! This greatly puzzled the refitting yard, since destroyer Captains are generally only too anxious to have all traces of damage, especially from collisions, obliterated; but for Baker-Cresswell the dent had special significance.

By 6.50 p.m. U.110 was safely in tow again, and the *Bulldog* set course for Iceland with the damaged *Broadway* as escort. Baker-Cresswell now told Smith of the *Aubrietia*, who had done such excellent work that day, to transfer the prisoners to the *Amazon*, take the *Nigella* under his wing and make for the rendezvous with the east-bound convoy (HX.124), which was the 3rd Escort Group's next responsibility. We have already seen how they set out on that duty, and need only note that they successfully met the new convoy two nights later—both ships very short of depth charges.

Once he was well clear of the position where he had seized his prize Baker-Cresswell felt it safe to break wireless silence, and tell the Admiralty that he had captured U.110, that all her books, logs, charts and movable equipment were onboard his ship, that he was towing her towards Iceland and that he urgently needed help from submarine experts.

In Whitehall the message caused no little stir. It was at

once taken to the Director of Intelligence and the First Sea Lord, and the latter ordered that the circulation of the news was to be restricted to a very few selected officers. He replied to the *Bulldog* that the operation of recovering the U-boat was to be given the code-name " Primrose," and that all mention of it was to be graded " Top Secret."[1] To that message Admiral Noble added another a short while later, saying that a Sunderland flying boat was taking off immediately with submarine experts on board. At the time when Baker-Cresswell received this message, about midnight, it might still have been possible for a flying boat to alight on the open sea; but it would have been a risky business, and so rapidly were wind and sea rising that there seemed little prospect of doing so next morning.

Before turning in Baker-Cresswell had another look at his prize. She was riding quite easily, though perhaps a little more down by the stern. He had gradually worked up speed from 4 to 5, then 6, and finally to $7\frac{1}{2}$ knots. Yet he was still nearly 400 miles from his destination—at least 50 hours' steaming. Two whole days? Could she possibly stay afloat that length of time? Nor was that the only doubt and anxiety to assail his mind. The *Broadway*, many of whose fuel tanks had been damaged when she rammed U.110, reported that she could only just reach Iceland; and, still worse, was the inevitable doubt as to whether he had done the right thing. The convoy, which was his primary responsibility, had taken several nasty knocks before he had left it; and he suspected that it had since been attacked again. As he stretched out on the charthouse settee the explicit wording of the Admiralty's

[1] The fact that the corvette *Primrose* took part in the defence of OB.318 in the 7th Escort Group, and that Group Captain Primrose was in command of the Iceland-based aircraft of Coastal Command which co-operated in the protection of the convoy, makes the choice of code-name appear rather a curious coincidence; but it is likely that it was only a coincidence.

instructions to Escort Commanders rang in his tired brain. "The safe and timely arrival of the convoy . . . is the primary object, and nothing relieves the escort commander of his responsibility in this respect." Nothing ? Not even the capture of a U-boat? Baker-Cresswell wondered how his disregard of that ancient principle would be taken—especially if he failed to get the prize in. "Well," he thought, "other officers have disobeyed orders, and been abundantly justified for doing so. Perhaps . . ."; and for a few hours he dropped into the deep sleep of exhaustion.

CHAPTER IX

Disaster—and Triumph

As DUSK started to close down on the convoy on 9th May Commodore Mackenzie was reviewing the dilemma that faced him as anxiously as Baker-Cresswell, then about 70 miles away to the north-east, was considering his own quite different predicament. Only two escorts, the *Hollyhock* and the *Daneman*, were still with the merchantmen. The *Aubrietia* and *Nigella*, after taking part in the hunts for U.110 and 201, had been detached to make for the rendezvous with their next convoy; the *Amazon* (which was short of fuel and out of depth charges) was on her way to Iceland with the prisoners, the *Angle* had long since had to leave because of fuel shortage, the *St. Apollo* was standing by the *Empire Cloud*, and the damaged *Broadway* was struggling towards her base whilst providing what protection she could to the *Bulldog*. Mackenzie had now reached the meridian of 34° West, which was little short of the position which the Admiralty had originally laid down as the convoy's dispersal point; and that morning a signal had come through from Admiral Noble ordering the convoy to disperse at daylight on 10th, the escorts remaining " in loose company " for the rest of that day. But the Commander-in-Chief could hardly have known that only two small escort vessels were actually still with the convoy. Might it not therefore be better for the Commodore to use his discretionary powers and disperse the convoy at dusk that evening, so giving the merchantmen the benefit of the shield of darkness for the first few hours of their lonely voyages towards their various destinations? On the other hand the night was not likely to be very dark, for a nearly full moon would shed a good deal of light on the sea, even though the sky was now mostly overcast and the horizon misty. Other U-boats might well be shadowing the convoy, and with the visibility as great as three or four miles dispersal might help them to find easy targets. Mackenzie therefore decided that on balance it was better to keep the convoy in formation; but if any other attack took place he would at once order it to disperse. This latter decision certainly seems open to question, since all our recent experience had proved that, even if the escort was very weak, it was far better for merchant ships to remain in convoy. Mackenzie now had only 33 ships under his charge, and after the many alarms of the previous afternoon they had settled down on course South 60° West (true) with the *Ranpura* still in position between Columns 5 and 6. At midnight the Commodore altered 50 degrees to port as an evasive measure, and maintained that course until 2.20 a.m. on the 10th, when he wheeled the convoy to South 40° West (true). These measures were not, however, to save his charges from another enemy who, quite unknown to him, had overtaken his convoy and was now poised and ready to strike new blows.

When Kapitänleutnant Herbert Wohlfarth of U.556 intercepted the shadowing reports sent by U.110 and 201 on the 9th, he at once set course to intercept the convoy. That afternoon and evening he dived regularly to listen for propeller noises on his hydrophones, and at 2 a.m. next morning he was rewarded by obtaining a clear bearing of such sounds. He surfaced, and found himself on the starboard bow of the convoy, which, as far as he could tell, had only one " destroyer " (actually the corvette *Hollyhock*) protecting it. The night was fairly light, but clouds periodically obscured the moon; and this and an increasingly rough sea made it easier for him to approach unobserved. He therefore decided to attack on the surface, and at 2.42 a.m. fired two torpedoes at ships

whose size he estimated as 8,000 and 5,000 tons. He claimed
that he hit them both, but in fact one torpedo struck the
Aelybryn (No. 93), which was now the only ship remaining
in the ill-fated starboard wing column of the convoy[1], and the
other missed. For some unexplained reason the Dutch ship
Hercules (No. 83) now sent out a submarine attack report.
Possibly she thought that she herself had been struck; but her
message was picked up by Cuba radio, and also by several
stations in Britain; and that evening Bremen wireless station
very kindly broadcasted " In English for England " that
" The Dutch freighter *Hercules* of 2,317 tons has been torpedoed
in the Atlantic." The German propaganda service certainly
worked quickly; but in this case its information was wrong,
as the *Hercules* never suffered any damage at all. A good
many hours elapsed, however, before either the Commodore
or Lieutenant Davies of the *Hollyhock*, let alone the naval
authorities at home, sorted out which ship had actually been
hit.

As soon as he heard the new torpedo explosion the Commodore ordered yet another emergency turn to port. Since
first exercising that manœuvre off the Butt of Lewis five days
earlier the convoy had executed literally dozens of such
turns. The *Chaucer* (No. 82) which was ahead of the *Hercules*
and very close to the *Aelybryn* did not, however, wait for that
order, but carried out a very prompt independent manœuvre.
Her Master had noted that in every previous attack two ships
had been struck, and he realised that his own position was
now particularly vulnerable. He therefore fired a rocket,
put his helm hard-a-starboard and went ahead at full speed.
As his ship was swinging round a torpedo passed a short
distance ahead of her. It is thus plain that the *Chaucer* was
the second ship at which Wohlfarth fired, and that only

[1] According to Commodore Mackenzie's report. If he was
correct the *Nailsea Manor*, originally No. 94, must have changed
her position in the convoy. See Map 6 (p. 144).

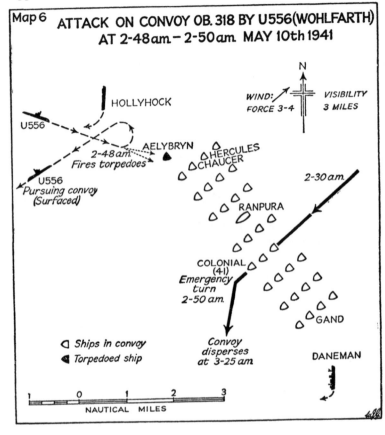

Map 6 ATTACK ON CONVOY OB.318 BY U556(WOHLFARTH)
AT 2·48am – 2·50am MAY 10th 1941

HOLLYHOCK

WIND:
FORCE 3-4

VISIBILITY
3 MILES

U556

AELYBRYN

HERCULES
CHAUCER

2-48am
Fires torpedoes

U556
Pursuing convoy
(Surfaced)

2-30a.m.

RANPURA

COLONIAL
(41)
Emergency
turn
2-50a.m.

GAND

◁ Ships in convoy
◀ Torpedoed ship

Convoy
disperses
at 3-25 am

DANEMAN

0   1   2   3
NAUTICAL   MILES

her Master's alertness saved her. Meanwhile the *Hollyhock*
was coming round from her position on the starboard beam of
the convoy to search on the quarter and to the rear of it;
but she could not obtain any sign of the attacker. The *Daneman*,
which had already done such excellent rescue work in the
earlier attacks, at once closed the *Aelybryn* and picked up not
only her Master, Captain H. W. Brockwell, and his entire
crew of 44, but all the 52 survivors of the *Gregalia* who were

on board the ship, and now had the experience of being torpedoed twice in the same convoy. The little *Daneman* thus had no less than 175 survivors from three different ships (*Eastern Star*, *Gregalia*, and *Aelybryn*) onboard her. Where she managed to put them all, and how she fed them is not recorded. Evidently her skipper, Lieutenant A. H. Ballard, R.N.R., regarded it all as part of the day's work, for he seems never to have rendered any report on the adventures of his ship while escorting OB.318. Captain Brockwell, however, reported that he and his men " were treated with the utmost consideration."

After his first attack was completed Wohlfarth withdrew from the convoy to reload his torpedo tubes and signal his report. His wireless office was listening on the normal mercantile wavelength (600 metres) and so picked up the *Hercules's* incorrect report. Apparently he never knew the actual results of his attack. When reloading was completed he closed the convoy again, but found it too light for his liking, and therefore decided to draw ahead and postpone his next attack until a more favourable opportunity offered.

At 3.11 a.m. Commodore Mackenzie carried out another emergency turn to port, and as there were now no escorts at all with the convoy, at 3.25 he made the signal to disperse. The position was 60°12' North 34° 30' West; but that, unfortunately, was not quite the end of the troubles suffered by the ships of OB.318, to whom we will return again shortly.

At daylight Captain Brockwell and some of the *Daneman's* crew returned to the *Aelybryn* to estimate the chances of salving her. They found that, although her rudder and propeller had been blown away, and there was water in the engine and boiler rooms, the main bulkheads appeared to be sound. The *Hollyhock*, which was also standing by the damaged ship, therefore signalled to Admiral Noble asking that a tug should be sent. To that the Commander-in-Chief replied that the *Hollyhock* was to continue to stand by the *Aelybryn* until the tug arrived, but the *Daneman* was to be sent straight to Iceland to land her many rescued merchant seamen. Four days later the *Zwarte Zee*, which had originally left England with OB.318 but had been detached to Iceland on 7th May[1], located the damaged ship and took her in tow. Escorted by the *Hollyhock* they arrived safely in Reykjavik on the 17th, and thus was another fine merchantman salved and repaired to continue in Allied service.

We must now continue with the story of the other merchantmen. In the half light of dawn Wohlfarth saw that the convoy had dispersed, and his hopes of collecting some easy victims rose; but the visibility was indifferent, and at first he could not make out any ships distinctly. Suddenly he sighted a single ship coming up from astern. He dived at once, fired two torpedoes as she steamed into his sights, and saw her sink very quickly indeed. His new victim was the *Empire Caribou*, which had set a westerly course from the dispersal point, to discharge her cargo of chalk at Portland, Maine. At 4.45 a.m. she was struck by two torpedoes in quick succession and sank in about two minutes.[2] Some of her crew of 45 managed to get away on rafts; but their experience was a terrible one, as the sea was now fairly rough and no rescue ship was in sight. Thirty-eight hours later the destroyer *Malcolm*, one of the ships sent to search the scene of the disaster, found eleven exhausted men on rafts and an overturned lifeboat. The ship's carpenter was picked up alive holding on to a crate; but not one deck officer survived. In casualties it was by far the worst blow suffered by the ships of OB.318, which had until then been extremely fortunate in that respect. Nor

---

[1] See p. 61.

[2] There is an unusually large discrepancy of times here. Wohlfarth says he sighted the *Empire Caribou* at 5.17 a.m. (G.M.T.) and fired at her at 5.32. British records say she was hit at 4.45. It may well be that the German times are in this case the more accurate.

was that the end; for Wohlfarth had only withdrawn to reload again, and at 6 a.m. he resumed the pursuit of the dispersed ships. His next attack, however, failed. He fired at a zigzagging merchantman at 9.17, but did not realise until too late that she was in ballast and high out of the water. The torpedo probably passed under her, but no ship reported the attack. Wohlfarth then reloaded once more, surfaced and steered to the south-west. At 3.30 p.m. he sighted two more ships, one of which was zig-zagging while the other was steering a straight course. He decided to attack the latter, actually the Belgian ship *Gand*, which had stopped zig-zagging because she believed herself to be clear of the danger zone. Just before 6 p.m. Wohlfarth fired a torpedo which struck her beneath the bridge and brought her to a stop with a heavy list; but she remained afloat. The U-boat commander circled her, watching through his periscope, and saw the crew abandon ship; but he had no intention of letting her escape. At 7.20 he therefore came to the surface and sank her by gunfire, while her crew looked on helplessly from the lifeboats. They declared later that he had also shelled the boats, but it seems unlikely that this was deliberate. More probably some shots which missed the ship fell near them, and gave the impression that they were being fired at. In his own account Wohlfarth merely states how he dealt the ship her death blow. After this success he was unable to continue the pursuit because he was having trouble with his air compressor, and was unable to rectify it while running on his diesel engines. He therefore turned back to the north-east, looking for stragglers. Happily he found none.

Though on this occasion Wohlfarth profited skilfully from the dispersal of the convoy, U.556 did not survive long afterwards. On her very next cruise, when operating against the homeward-bound convoy HX.133 to the south of Greenland on 27th June, she was forced to the surface and sunk by the escorting corvettes' depth charges. Wohlfarth himself was picked up, and passed the rest of the war in a prison camp.

In the early hours of 12th May, nearly two days after the sinking of the *Gand*, the destroyer *Burwell* found her boats and rescued 43 of her crew. Though we have no first-hand report from her survivors it appears that they had only one casualty. Their good fortune, compared with the fate of the *Empire Caribou*'s men, was doubtless due to their ship staying afloat long enough for them to get away from her in properly equipped lifeboats. Nor were these two ships the last of OB.318's number to fall victim to U-boats; for those which were bound to Freetown and more southerly ports still had to run the gauntlet of the U-boats which the Germans had sent to operate off the coast of Sierra Leone. Although there were never more than 6 or 7 present in those waters they found a great deal of unescorted traffic, and between the end of April and the middle of July 1941, they sank no less than 81 Allied merchantmen. We then managed to catch and sink the two supply ships *Egerland* and *Lothringen* on which the U-boats depended to prolong their cruises, and this, combined with the extension of convoy, brought a rapid decline in the enemy's successes. Unfortunately the merchantmen from OB.318 reached the dangerous waters at the height of the German successes. On the 23rd May the Dutch ship *Berhala* (originally No. 64 in the convoy), which had formerly been the Hamburg-Amerika Line's *Rheinland*, and had been captured in Sumatra in 1940, was sunk by U.38; and three days later Commodore Mackenzie's *Colonial* was hit by two torpedoes fired by U.107 when she was only 100 miles off Freetown. Her Master, Captain J. J. Devereux, sighted the U-boat quite close to him, and made a gallant endeavour to ram; but it was of no avail, and at 10 p.m. a third torpedo sank his ship. The Commodore and his staff got away on a raft, and all the rest of the 83 souls on board (including two injured men) were saved in the two port side boats, the starboard ones having been destroyed by the explosions. A wireless message was sent before the ship sank, but it was not until 20 hours later that the crew were picked up. The rescue ship was the old battleship *Centurion*, formerly wireless-controlled target ship for the fleet, which was then masquerading under the *nom-de-guerre* of H.M.S. *Anson* and had recently called at Gibraltar after escorting the carrier *Furious* from Britain with fighter aircraft which were to be flown on to Malta. In his report on the loss of his ship Captain Devereux told how " Sharks were jumping at the boats, and we beat them off with our oars. We had plenty of biscuits . . . and found them very eatable; but the water supply was very small." Luckily he and his men were rescued before suffering the worst tortures of thirst in open boats in the tropics. Commodore Mackenzie lost all his papers, and although on his return to England he pieced together a very good report from memory, it was inevitable that he should have been unable to recall many points of detail; and this has made it all the harder to reconstruct the journey of OB.318 with full accuracy. His experiences were, however, fairly typical of an Atlantic convoy of those days. Though strongly escorted and protected, and excellently disciplined in its own manœuvres, it lost four ships (23,539 tons) and had two others damaged while in convoy; and four more ships (21,777 tons) were sunk after they had dispersed. Thus of the 42 ships which sailed in the convoy (including the sections which left for and joined from Iceland) only 32 reached their destinations.

On 10th May Dönitz's staff at Lorient summarised the results of the various attacks on OB.318. They remarked that it had been " strongly escorted, was first reported by U.94, then by U.110, and was also attacked by U.201 and U.556." So far their entries were perfectly correct, but in assessing the results achieved they were fairly wide of the mark. The claims made, and the actual results achieved were as follows:—

U-boat	CLAIMED SINKINGS		ACTUAL SINKINGS*		DAMAGED	
	Ships	*Tonnage*	*Ships*	*Tonnage*	*Ships*	*Tonnage*
U.94	4	20,000	2	15,901	—	—
U.110	3 or 4	18,248	2	7,638	—	—
U.201	2	18,000	1	5,802	1	5,968
U.556	3	20,000	2	10,047	1	4,986
TOTALS:	12 or 13	76,248	7	39,388	2	10,954

*These exclude the *Berhala* and *Colonial*, which
were sunk by other U-boats much later.

The U-boat command staff continued in their War Diary
for 10th May with the remark that they " received many air
and U-boat reports on this day." They concluded that the
British " do not keep to certain convoy routes, but disperse
their traffic over a wide area "; and that " they do not on
principle avoid areas where sinkings by U-boats have occurred."
Finally they noted, correctly, that " U.110 gave no position
report as requested, and must be considered lost."

On the same evening that Dönitz's staff thus summarised
the attacks on OB.318, the Admiralty sent a message to all
authorities telling them that the convoy had dispersed, and
giving the expected times of arrival of each ship at its destination. That signal might be expected to mark the end of the
story of our particular convoy; but such is not the case. For
the next week the aftermath of its adventures figured promi-
nently in the Admiralty's signal files, and those messages
provide us with a very clear picture of how our world-wide
shipping control organisation worked. There we can see the
Western Approaches Command and its subordinate authorities
organising the salvage and towage of the damaged ships, the
Naval Control Service Staff in the overseas ports signalling
the arrival of each merchantman and particulars of the
survivors disembarked; we hear the *Malcolm* report over the

ether that she had found the few survivors from the *Empire Caribou*; the Flag Officer in Charge, Iceland, signals the return to base of each warship engaged on the operation; and finally the same authority gives Admiral Noble the experiences gained in the four attacks on the convoy. Nor should it be thought that this process was being carried out for one convoy only; for an equally careful watch was in fact being kept on at least a dozen others which were crossing the Atlantic, homeward or outward, at the same time as OB.318.

We left Baker-Cresswell's *Bulldog* steering towards Reykjavik at midnight on 9th–10th May with U.110 towing satisfactorily; but the sea and wind continued to rise during the night, and by the time that dawn broke it was blowing so strongly that the U-boat started to yaw badly, and it had become impossible to hold her on a steady course. She was, moreover still more down by the stern, and had begun to labour badly. At 7 a.m. Baker-Cresswell decided that he must heave to, keeping the towing wire barely taut, and allowing the U-boat to head down wind. On the *Bulldog*'s bridge every man's stomach felt as though it was filled with lead; but their suspense was at any rate not very prolonged, for at 10.50 a.m. U.110 suddenly and defiantly reared her bows up into the air till they were nearly vertical. She then slowly sank until the only sign of her was the wire trailing in the *Bulldog*'s wake. When it tautened out the men on the quarterdeck knocked off the slip by which it was secured to the ship, and as the end splashed into the water all their hopes seemed to have gone overboard with it. But, although, they did not know it at the time, what they already had on board their ship was far more valuable than the U-boat's empty hull could have been.

Baker-Cresswell at once signalled his bad news to Admiral Noble, and set course for Reykjavik at 20 knots. He arrived there at 11 p.m. that evening with only a few tons of fuel remaining. Early next morning the *Amazon* reached Hvalfiord with the prisoners. Meanwhile the Admiralty had ordered

Baker-Cresswell himself to take over the prisoners, and proceed to Scapa Flow with all despatch. The *Bulldog* therefore refuelled during the night, collected the prisoners from the *Amazon* and set course for Scapa early on the 11th at 25 knots. On the way round Baker-Cresswell spoke to his ship's company about the need for absolute secrecy regarding what they had seen, and he had his own ship searched for any tell-tale signs of the capture she had made. After he had given permission for the Germans to come on deck for exercise he suddenly saw a boat hook which was plainly not of British pattern, and had actually been brought back from U.110. He had it hastily put out of sight, and none of the Germans noticed it. While on passage to Scapa Baker-Cresswell had a long talk with Loewe on the *Bulldog*'s bridge, in his halting German and his erstwhile enemy's much better English. To his great relief he found that all the German survivors were completely convinced that their ship had sunk very soon after they had abandoned her. Loewe would hear nothing said against the Nazi régime, and was confident that he would be shot on reaching England. He plainly disbelieved Baker-Cresswell's assurance that, on the contrary, he would be accommodated in a country mansion, where he would spend the rest of the war in far greater comfort than his British captors could hope to enjoy.

On the afternoon of 12th May the *Bulldog* passed through the Scapa boom defences, and then secured to an oiler. Two representatives from the Admiralty, who had flown north to take over the captured trophies, at once came aboard. They had brought with them small briefcases in which they apparently expected to carry back a few papers. When they saw the two large packing-cases in the Captain's cabin full of books, documents and equipment their eyes nearly popped out of their heads. " What ! " said one of them, handling a trophy, " this . . . ? And this . . . ? We've waited a long time for one of these ! " Far into the night worked the experts, to make certain that no item was deteriorating due to damp. When they left one of them said, " Never mind about losing U.110. From our point of view it is a good thing. Not a word about this to a single soul—except of course the C.-in-C."; and Baker-Cresswell then knew that the blow which had seemed to strike him between the eyes as his prize slid beneath the waves two days earlier had been an illusion.

Next day Baker-Cresswell lunched with Admiral Sir John Tovey, the Commander-in-Chief, Home Fleet, in his flagship the *King George V*, and told his story. The Admiral listened quietly and then said, " You fellows get all the fun. I just stay here and wait for the enemy to come out. It's a dull job. Sometimes I sits and thinks, and sometimes I just sits." Little did he then know that, ten days later, he and his whole fleet would be at sea in pursuit of the *Bismarck* and *Prinz Eugen*. That night a message from the First Sea Lord, originated at 11.10 p.m. reached Baker-Cresswell. " Hearty congratulations," it said, " the petals of your flower are of rare beauty." One can visualise Sir Dudley Pound, sitting at his big desk overlooking the Horseguards' Parade, at the end of another long and tiring day, writing out that message in his own hand after hearing from the Director of Intelligence what the 3rd Escort Group had achieved.

At the time the great value of the service performed by the 3rd Escort Group was fully realised in high circles. Baker-Cresswell's name appeared in the next list of promotions from Commander to Captain, and the Admiralty was also generous in the matter of recommendations for decorations. In due course Baker-Cresswell and Smith were gazetted Companions of the Distinguished Service Order; Taylor, Dodds and Balme were awarded the Distinguished Service Cross; Chief Stoker Capelin of the *Broadway*, Telegraphist Long of the *Bulldog*, and Able Seaman Rutledge of the *Aubrietia* received Distinguished Service Medals, and 14 officers and men were " Mentioned in Dispatches." Dodds remembers that, at the investiture at which he received his D.S.C., King George VI told him that the operation in which he had gained it was perhaps the most important single event in the whole war at sea; which shows how much the monarch knew about what went on in the service to which he himself had devoted so much of his early life, and which always retained his deep affection. When the reports on the operation reached Admiral Noble he forwarded them to the Admiralty with the comment that " Commander Baker-Cresswell has worked up the 3rd Escort Group to good efficiency, and a fine spirit prevails." That, though undoubtedly true, hardly expressed the real reasons for his recommendations. Those have, until now, been perhaps the best kept secret of the whole war. So well kept was his secret that when, nine years later, Baker-Cresswell received a letter from the Admiralty telling him that he was to be placed on the Retired List, and thanking him for his past services to the Navy, not a word was said about the most outstanding accomplishment of his whole career.

Epilogue

BAKER-CRESSWELL returned to Iceland in his *Bulldog* during the night following his interview with Admiral Tovey. Two days later he had collected the 3rd Escort Group and was at sea again on his way to meet the slow homeward convoy SC.31. The mid-ocean groups were never allowed much rest during the difficult months of 1941. On 21st May he met the convoy in 40° West, about the longitude of Cape Farewell in Greenland; for the recent appearance of U-boats so much farther out into the Atlantic had forced our escorts to extend their protecting shield. On the present occasion Admiralty intelligence estimated that no less than nine enemies were searching for the convoy, and as Baker-Cresswell had only six of his group with him he felt distinctly uncomfortable. But it was not, in fact, the U-boats which were to menace these new charges of the 3rd Escort Group; for on the very day that Baker-Cresswell met his convoy, the *Bismarck* and *Prinz Eugen* sailed on their Atlantic foray. By the evening of 23rd May, when our patrolling cruisers sighted them in the Denmark Strait, the convoy had reached a point directly in the path of the powerful German squadron, whose progress Baker-Cresswell was able to plot from the reports of the shadowing warships. He was not, however, unduly anxious; for he knew that the *Hood* was in the vicinity, and his thought was " It will be all right—the *Hood* will surely fix them." Then came a signal stating that the *Bismarck* had sunk the battle cruiser—news which the escort commander at first simply could not credit. He had dined on board that magnificent ship, which the Royal Navy had regarded with pride and affection ever since she had first entered service in the early 1920s, only a few days earlier when in Hvalfiord. Surely, he thought, they must have got the name of the sunken ship wrong?

During the early hours of 24th May the visibility, which has been extreme, began to close down, and Baker-Cresswell knew that his convoy might be steering into acute danger. What could he do? Although most of the Western Approaches destroyers had landed their torpedo tubes in order to reduce top-weight and enable them to carry more depth charges, he had refused to have them removed from the *Bulldog*. Now he was glad of that decision; for his was the only destroyer anywhere near the formidable enemy. The weather conditions seemed ideal for torpedo attack, and he therefore broke wireless silence to ask permission to join in the chase; but his Commander-in-Chief ordered him to remain with the convoy. By this time the enemy was only 50 miles away, so the escort commander organised his group to prepare to cover the convoy with smoke and engage the most powerful warship afloat. Happily the *Bismarck* altered course to the west at the critical moment—we now know that she was striving her utmost to shake off the cruisers which were shadowing her so pertinaciously—and so passed a short distance astern of the convoy. The story of how the Admiralty then drew an ever-tightening net around the fleeing warship, for Admiral Tovey to sink her far away to the south-east early on 27th May has passed into history. We may be thankful that the *Bulldog* and her consorts, who had so recently made such an important contribution to the British victory at sea, were not called on to sacrifice themselves in a hopeless fight against vastly superior odds; but the Group's records show that they were fully prepared to do so.

INDEX

Index

Index

Index

Index

DIAGRAM 3

CONVOY OB. 318

FORMATION ON SAILING 2nd MAY 1941

(Not to scale)

Column 1	*Column 2*	*Column 3*	*Column 4*	*Column 5*
△	△		▲	△
11. TUREBY	21. BRITISH PRINCE	31.(VACANT)	41. COLONIAL	51. CITY OF
(BRIT., 4372)	(BRIT., 4979)		(BRIT, 5108)	KIMBERLE
	<u>Vice-Commodore's ship</u>		<u>Commodore's ship</u> (Sunk May 26th after dispersal)	(BRIT., 6169)
▲	△	△	△	△
12. GAND	22. EDAM	32. SOMMERSTAD	42.CITY OF CAIRO	52. LUCERN
(BEL.,5186)	(DUTCH, 8871)	(NORW, TANKER 5923)	(BRIT., 8034)	(BRIT., TANKE 6556)
(Sunk May 10th after dispersal)				
△	△	△	▲	△
13. HOYANGER	23. AGIOI VICTORES	33. BARON CAWDOR	43. EASTERN STAR	53. EL MIRL(
(NORW., 4624)	(GREEK. 4344)	(BRIT., 3638)	(NORW., 5638) (Sunk May 7th)	(BRIT, TANK 8092)
△	△	△	△	▲
14. NEW YORK CITY	24. LIMA	34. KING EDWIN	44. ATLANTIC COAST	54. IXION
(BRIT., 2710)	(SWEDE, 5244)	(BRIT., 4536)	(BRIT., 890)	(BRIT.,10,263 (Sunk May 7
	△	△		△
15. (VACANT)	25. ORMINSTER	35. ATHELSULTAN	45.(VACANT)	55. BEN LOMO
	(BRIT., 5712)	(BRIT., TANKER, 8882)		(BRIT.,6630)

........Sunk Ships

........Damaged Ships

Column 6	*Column 7*	*Column 8*	*Column 9*

61. BURMA
(BRIT., 7821)
<u>*Rear-Commodore's ship*</u>

71. BENGORE HEAD
(BRIT., 2609)
(Sunk May 9th)

81. EMPIRE CARIBOU
(BRIT., 4861)
(Sunk May 10th after dispersal)

91. ESMOND
(BRIT., 5029)
(Sunk May 9th)

62. GYDA
BRIT., 1695)

72. GREGALIA
(BRIT., 5802)
(Sunk May 9th)

82. CHAUCER
(BRIT., 5792)

92. EMPIRE CLOUD
(BRIT., 5968)
(Torpedoed May 9th towed in)

ANPURA
joining
om Iceland)

63. *(VACANT)*

73. *(VACANT)*

83. HERCULES
(DUTCH, 2317)

93. AELYBRYN
(BRIT., 4986)
(Torpedoed May 10th towed in)

64. BERHALA
(DUTCH, 6622)
(Sunk May 24th after dispersal)

74. NAGINA
(BRIT., 6551)

84. TORNUS
(BRIT., TANKER 8054)

94. NAILSEA MANOR
(BRIT., 4926)

65. IRON BARON
(BRIT., 4584)

75. ZWARTE ZEE
(DUTCH TUG, 793)

85. *(VACANT)*

95. *(VACANT)*